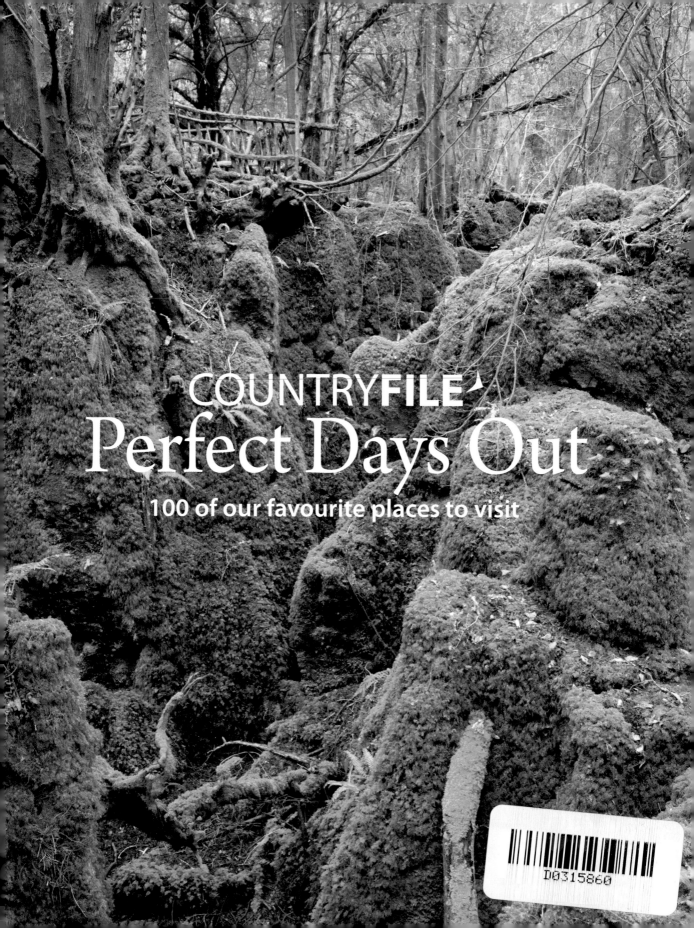

COUNTRY**FILE**
Perfect Days Out
100 of our favourite places to visit

COUNTRY**FILE**

Perfect Days Out

100 of our favourite places to visit

CAVAN SCOTT

Cavan Scott launched *Countryfile Magazine* in 2007, working with the team of the popular television show to produce a new magazine that would celebrate the great British countryside. Passionate about British countryside and wildlife, he is a judge of various countryside awards including the RSPB Farming for Nature Award and the FARMA Farm Retailer of the Year.

ACKNOWLEDGEMENTS

A big thank you to Andrew Thorman, Teresa Bogan, Andrew Tomlinson, Barbara Lewis and Stephen Lockwood on the *Countryfile* TV team, and especially Andrea Buffery for putting up with my endless phone calls and emails.

Thanks also to Matt, Julia and John for finding the time to share their favourite locations and their help in compiling our 100 perfect days.

Big rounds of applause to my editors Laura Higginson and Muna Reyal for their support, advice and creativity throughout the entire project.

And, finally, massive hugs to my lovely wife, Clare, and gorgeous girls, Chloe and Connie, for their patience and love while I was hammering away at a keyboard. This book is for you.

This book is published to accompany the television series entitled *Countryfile*, broadcast on BBC1.

Executive Editor: Andrew Thorman

10 9 8 7 6 5 4 3 2 1

Published in 2010 by BBC Books, an imprint of Ebury Publishing. A Random House Group Company

Text © Cavan Scott 2010
Design © Woodlands Books 2010

The Random House Group Limited
Reg. No. 954009

Addresses for companies within the Random House Group can be found at:
www.randomhouse.co.uk

A CIP catalogue record for this book is available from the British Library.

ISBN 978 1 84990 007 2

Mixed Sources
Product group from well-managed forests and other controlled sources
www.fsc.org Cert no. SGS-COC-005091
© 1996 Forest Stewardship Council
FSC

The Random House Group Limited supports the Forest Stewardship Council (FSC), the leading international forest certification organisation. All our titles that are printed on Greenpeace approved FSC certified paper carry the FSC logo. Our paper procurement policy can be found at www.rbooks.co.uk/environment.

Commissioning editor: Muna Reyal
Project editor: Laura Higginson
Copy-editor: Stephanie Evans
Designer: Alison Fenton
Picture researcher: Clare Limpus
Maps: John Dear

Colour origination, printed and bound in Great Britain by Butler Tanner & Dennis Ltd, Frome

To buy books by your favourite authors and register for offers, visit www.rbooks.co.uk

Page 1: the scowles in Puzzlewood, Forest of Dean; page 2-3: the view out to sea from Porlock Weir in Somerset.

Contents

❯ Introduction

On 24 July 1988, BBC1 viewers were treated to a new Sunday-morning programme that aimed to bring a little of the countryside into the nation's living rooms. *Countryfile* was born.

For over 20 years *Countryfile* has explored the Great British countryside, visiting some of the most beautiful landscapes the United Kingdom has to offer. Today over six million viewers tune in every week to watch a team of presenters, led by Matt Baker, Julia Bradbury and John Craven, explore our national rural treasures and seek out little-known gems. It's easy to see why: amazing stories, fantastic characters and spectacular locations. In other words, essential viewing.

But watching *Countryfile* is only half of the story. If you think the scenery is stunning on your small screen, seeing it in the flesh will simply blow you away. No top-of-the-range, high-definition, widescreen television can ever compare with the view you get from the summit of Snowdon or turning to see the jagged limestone outcrops of the Yorkshire Dales rolling out before you.

That's where this book comes in. We've picked 100 of *Countryfile*'s favourite locations. It wasn't easy. Our countryside has a veritable embarrassment of riches and the problem was never what are we going to include but what are we going to leave out? Those locations, attractions and areas that made our final list are just the tip of the haystack. You'll find everything from majestic hills and verdant valleys to sleepy villages and bustling market towns. Relics of our feudal, religious and industrial heritage dot the landscape as you travel by road, rail or waterway. There's history to discover, new tastes to sample and wonderful wildlife to experience. Then there's the gamut of weird and wonderful traditions that take place throughout the year, from village-wide rugby scrums like the Haxey Hood to bizarre contests such as the World Stinging Nettle Eating Championships. Along the way you'll also hear from

Matt, Julia and John as they pick out their own top locations and give us a behind-the-scenes look at the filming of the nation's most popular countryside TV show.

If this is all new to you, then I'm actually quite jealous. What amazing adventures lie ahead as you discover for yourself what joys the countryside can bring. And the good news is that there's always something new to discover. I hope that even the most dyed-in-wool country-dweller will find unknown treasures tucked away in these pages, a place they never knew existed or a story they've yet to hear.

Each location has been chosen as somewhere you can visit in a day. Some are dedicated tourist attractions, while others are general areas to choose from or specific journeys to make. Where possible, we've included postcodes for those setting out with a GPS system in their car or details of the local bus and railway services if you're relying on local transport. Of course, it isn't always possible just to step off a bus or train when visiting the countryside, so it's worth looking up the websites and tourist-information details given to check whether you'll have a little way to walk or to confirm that the particular attraction is open on the day you're visiting.

Oh, and there's something else you should prepare yourself for. The British countryside is positively addictive. Start exploring and you won't want to stop. Every inch of every hectare is soaked in history and legend. There's tranquillity and drama at each turn, sights that take your breath away and beauty that stirs your soul. Once it's possessed you, you'll become greedy for it, wanting to find out more, to protect it and understand how it works.

It's your countryside. Get out there and enjoy it.

Cavan Scott

Kingsgate beach on the Isle of Thanet (opposite); Hathersage Moor in the Dark Peak area of the Peak District (above).

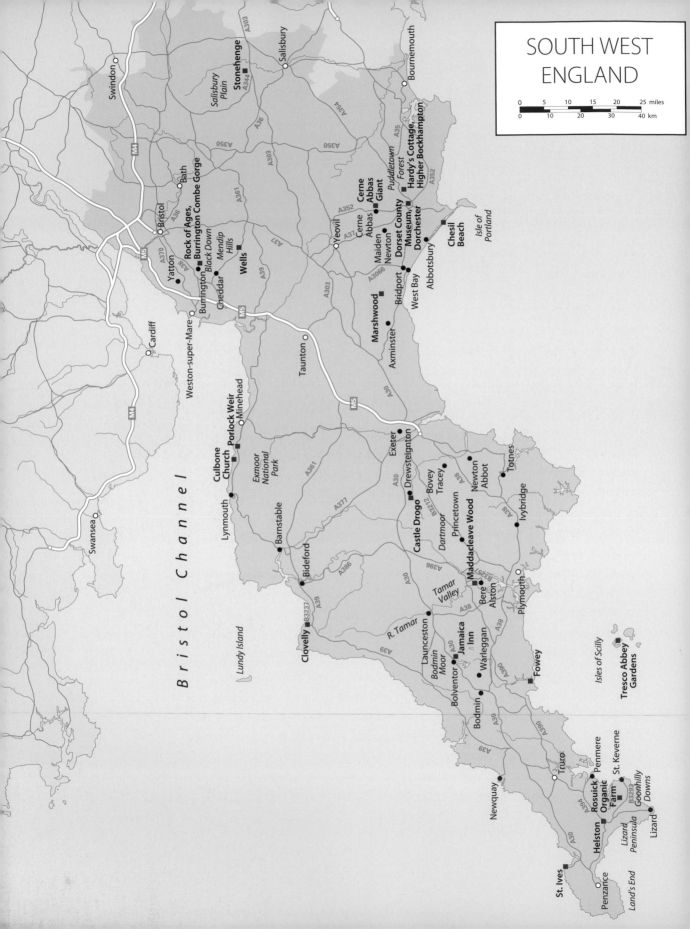

0   5   10   15   20   25 miles
0   10   20   30   40 km

Swindon

A303

Salisbury
A344 Stonehenge

Salisbury
Plain
A36
A303
A350
A354

Bournemouth

Puddletown
Forest Hardy's Cottage,
Higher Bockhampton
A35
A352

Bath
A36
Rock of Ages,
Burrington Combe Gorge
Cerne
Abbas
Giant
A361 Burrington Black Down
Mendip
Hills
Cerne
Abbas
Dorset County
Museum,
Dorchester
Isle of
Portland

Bristol
A370
Yatton
A38
Cheddar
Wells
A39
Yeovil
A37
Maiden
Newton
A3066
Chesil
Beach

Cardiff
Weston-super-Mare
Abbotsbury

M5
Bridport West Bay

Marshwood

Taunton
A30
Axminster

Swansea
M4

B r i s t o l   C h a n n e l

Porlock Weir
Culbone
Church Minehead

Exmoor
National
Park
A361
A377
A30

Exeter
Drewsteignton Bovey
Tracey Newton
Abbot
Totnes

Lynmouth
Castle Drogo
B3212
Dartmoor Princetown
A38
Maddacleave Wood Ivybridge

Barnstable

Bideford
A386
A386
Tamar
Valley Bere
Alston
Plymouth

Lundy Island
A39
R. Tamar
A38

Clovelly B3237
Launceston
Jamaica
Inn
Warleggan
Fowey

Isles of Scilly

Bodmin
Moor
Bolventor
A30
Bodmin
A30
A390
Tresco Abbey
Gardens

Newquay
A39
A38
A390

Truro

Penmere
Rosuick
Organic
Farm St. Keverne
B3293 Goonhilly
Downs

St. Ives
Helston
Lizard
Peninsula
Lizard

Penzance
A30
A394
Land's End

South West

The South West of England is steeped in mystery and myth. We will never know why a randy giant was carved into a hill in Dorset or why Stonehenge was erected all those centuries ago. Did a 19th-century holy man really shelter from the storm in the Rock of Ages in Burrington Combe Gorge or smugglers find their own sanctuary in a lonely inn on Bodmin Moor?

There is folklore in the making to be found as well. What stories will people tell of the noble bustard, a bird once lost from the British Isles but now re-establishing itself with the help of conservationists on Salisbury Plain? Will they wonder if the locals of a pub near Marshwood really did feast on stinging nettles, or praise the efforts of the food heroes who fought to save the silver darlings of Clovelly? And what of the fabled sub-tropical paradise just a few miles from the Cornish coast?

The good news is that you don't have to wait for such stories to become the stuff of legend. You can experience them and create your own sagas right now.

Smuggler's rest

❯ JAMAICA INN, CORNWALL

How to get there:

Jamaica Inn is located halfway
between Bodmin and
Launceston, leaving the
A30 at Bolventor.
For sat nav users: PL15 7TS
Nearest railway station:
Bodmin Parkway (9 miles)
Bus services:
www.westerngreyhound.com
01637 871 871

Find out more:

www.jamaicainn.co.uk
0156 686 250

Other things to see:

Du Maurier fans should head
to the pretty port of Fowey on
the south coast of Cornwall for
the official Daphne du Maurier
festival, held every May.
For sat nav users: PL23 1ET
www.dumaurierfestival.co.uk
01726 879 500

Even on a bright day, walking across Bodmin Moor is an awesome experience. This is a wild landscape, home to prehistoric stones and the ruins of Cornwall's traditional tin mines. It is also the setting for the novelist Daphne Du Maurier's darkest work. *Jamaica Inn* (1936) is a story of intrigue, vice and murder, its characters as bleak and twisted as Bodmin Moor itself. Today, the 400-year-old Jamaica Inn is a magnet for tourists, its sign squeaking eerily in the wind. Here you can sup a pint, wander around the slightly eccentric smugglers museum or even brave a night in one of its supposedly haunted rooms. Du Maurier lamented how her novel changed the nature of this remote drinking hole from an atmospheric, authentic inn to a full-on visitor attraction. And to think it was all by chance.

Du Maurier only discovered Jamaica Inn when riding one day with her friend Foy Quiller-Couch. An impenetrable fog swept in and the pair found themselves leading their horses through increasingly inclement weather. Then, out of the gloom, the chimneys of Jamaica Inn loomed into view.

Warming herself by the inn's roaring fire, Du Maurier eagerly listened to the legends of the moor, and the smugglers and wreckers who flashed lights from the shore to lure unwary skippers to their doom on the craggy Cornish coast. These tales formed the basis of her novel, although historians question whether smugglers really set foot in the pub, and whether wreckers existed at all. While shipwrecks were common, as were looters who

helped themselves to the cargo washed up on shore, there's no real evidence that rogues deliberately ran ships aground. However, Du Maurier's villain of the piece, the grotesque Vicar of Altarnun, was more factually accurate. He was based, in part, on Reverend Frederick Densham, who in 1931 became parish priest of Warleggan, east of Bodmin. When his eccentric nature drove his parishioners away, Densham preached to a congregation of cardboard cut-outs propped up in the pews. He shut himself off from the world and was found dead in the barricaded rectory in 1953.

Du Maurier set her sinister preacher in the real and attractive village of Altarnun, found just off the A30. Its Old Rectory, originally a Georgian mansion built in 1842, is now a hotel.

Clovelly in Devon
(previous page); the
Jamaica Inn sign and
old anchor resting
against the Inn wall hint
at a darker seafaring
past (right); Fowey
Harbour, Cornwall
(opposite).

Julia Bradbury on the best catch in St Ives »

I'm a real foodie but must admit I'm not too fond of really fishy fish. I've always considered mackerel to be too oily for me, but all that changed when we visited St Ives. I went out on a tiny fishing boat bagging hand-line-caught mackerel, taking our catch of around 30 fish to a local chef to barbecue it on the beach. He rustled up grilled mackerel with saffron and red onion jam and a tomato and mint salad on the side. It was delicious – subtle chunks of white melt-in-your-mouth flesh. I was converted on the spot, although I'll now only eat it fresh off the boat. If you're in Cornwall and have the chance to eat fresh line-caught mackerel, I'd jump at it if I were you.

Getting the hump
❯ THE LIZARD PENINSULA, CORNWALL

How to get there:

Take the B3293 from Helston to
St Keverne and look for signs for
Rosuick Organic Farm.
For sat nav users: TR12 6DZ
Nearest railway station:
Penmere (7 miles)
There is no bus service.

Find out more:

www.cornishcamels.com
01326 231 119

The Lizard Peninsula, England's most southernly point, is awash with history. It was from here that the Spanish Armada was first spotted in 1588, and down the centuries its sheltered coves and golden beaches were a smuggler's paradise, with resourceful free-traders landing barrels of contraband spirits and goods right under the noses of the Preventive boats that patrolled the dangerous waters. Many a ship was lost around this treacherous coastline and the famous lighthouse built in 1751 on Lizard Point still stands as a beacon for seafarers.

Today, the peninsula is a mecca for artists and wildlife enthusiasts. Cornwall's special light has attracted painters since the late 19th century, while the same sea-caves so prized by smugglers now provide a haven for grey seals that come ashore to pup between September and December.

While the Lizard has little to do with reptiles (its name comes from the Celtic *lys ardh* meaning 'high point'), in recent years you may find yourself face to face with an unexpected

newcomer to the Cornish countryside, one we associate more with deserts and date palms than granite and heather. Rosuick Organic Farm has long bred Welsh black cattle, Gloucester Old Spot and Dorset sheep. In 2004 farmer Christopher Oates decided to try his hand with a very different kind of beast – seven Bactrian camels imported from Kurdistan. They feed on hay and the farm's hedgerows, and receive a special winter supplement and neat salt. Between May and August, the herd, which now numbers 14, takes tourists trekking on the Goonhilly Downs to pay their way.

These ships of the desert have acclimatized well to their new home – except for their feet. Camels have nails and pads rather than hooves, and these can absorb water in Cornwall's wetter environment, so the herd gets a day off after taking a walk on the downs.

The Oates also have a good sideline in their new livestock. During summer, camels moult and the wool can be pulled off in handfuls and spun into yarn. Christopher has even had a number of celebrity chefs approach him to get hold of camel milk, but as yet he hasn't been able to milk the herd.

A view along the rugged coastline towards the lighthouse at Lizard Point.

Other things to see:
If you're visiting the Lizard around 8 May, get yourself to the town of Helston to witness the Flora or the Furry Dance, one of the oldest customs still practised in Britain. The place is festooned with flowers and four mass dances take place, including the main one at noon, which is performed in dignified formal dress. And count yourself lucky to witness the celebration – it was once banned by the Victorians for its 'drunken revelry'.
For sat nav users: TR13 8RB

Julia Bradbury on the Isles of Scilly »

I fell in love with the Isles of Scilly. They have a pace and style of life that is utterly idyllic and enviable. People are encouraged to leave their own transport on the mainland and rely on bicycle and water taxi to travel around the five inhabited islands. Every journey by water taxi only lasts up to 10 minutes and rush hour is wonderfully tranquil: no traffic lights or leaves on the line here!

It's not only people who take to the water. At the end of the Second World War heathland grazing started to diminish as the herds of cattle were removed from the islands. Soon the heathland became swamped with gorse and bracken. So, in the 80s, the Isles of Scilly Wildlife Trust brought a herd of Red Ruby cows back to the islands. I joined the Wildlife Trust team as they transported a year-old calf from St Mary's to Bryher, winching the nervous little fella onto a freight ship to transport him from island to island. That's what I call a real milk float!

Britain's sub-tropical paradise

❭ TRESCO ABBEY GARDENS, ISLES OF SCILLY

In the early 19th century Augustus Smith set out from Hertfordshire to find a worthy cause to satisfy his philanthropist nature. He didn't get far off the mainland. In 1834 he came to Tresco, one of over 150 granite islands that make up the Isles of Scilly. At the time, it was a forbidding place, far from the paradise that tourists enjoy today. Smith found barren plains whipped by fierce Atlantic gales. What little crops survived the wind and salt spray could never sustain the population. Smith secured a 99-year-long lease on the Isles of Scilly from the Duchy of Cornwall, paying £20,000 for the privilege, and styled himself as Lord Proprietor.

Part of his responsibilities to the Duchy was to improve the life of the islanders and so he promptly expelled members of the population he considered surplus to requirements. Then he planted gorse seeds and saplings around the islands. These grew into living windbreaks that provided essential protection for exposed farmland. Very soon daffodils were blooming, coming into flower much earlier owing to the Gulf Stream whose warm currents endow the islands with their mild, frost-free, climate. Smith was also responsible for building a quay at Hugh Town in order to export the flower crop to the mainland.

Some of Smith's decisions were revolutionary – he introduced compulsory education long before it existed in the rest of Britain – while others seemed highly questionable. Visitors to the island of Samson can explore the ruins of nine deserted cottages whose inhabitants were evicted by their Lord Proprietor to make room for a colony of deer. Unfortunately, for Smith, the deer had other ideas and promptly escaped Samson.

Smith's greatest legacy is found on Tresco, where he made his home. Around the ruins of a 12th-century Benedictine abbey he planted a series of Monterey and Norfolk Island pines, along with high hedges of holm oak as windbreaks. His simple but brilliant act transformed stark moorland into a vibrant sub-tropical garden that today shelters over 20,000 exotic plants from 80 countries in its 7 hectares (17 acres). Because temperatures rarely drop below 10°C, species from Australia and South Africa thrive in the dry terraces at the top of the gardens while others from more humid locations such as South America are planted near the bottom.

The four other islands of the archipelago that are inhabited reverted back to the Duchy in 1922, but Smith's descendants maintained the lease on Tresco and continue to develop their ancestor's sub-tropical paradise, just 28 miles from the Cornish coast.

How to get there:

Isles of Scilly helicopter:
www.islesofscillyhelicopter.com
01736 363 871
Scillonian III ferry (from Penzance) and Skybus plane (from Land's End or Newquay)
www.ios-travel.co.uk
0845 710 5555
For sat nav users: TR24 0QQ

Find out more:

www.tresco.co.uk
07817 971 327

Other things to see:

There have been more shipwrecks in the waters of the Isles of Scilly than almost anywhere else in the world. Augustus Smith salvaged 30 figureheads from 19th-century shipwrecks and these make up the Valhalla Collection found at the Tresco Abbey Gardens.

Balmy palms and other exotic flora transport you to foreign climes at the Tresco Abbey Gardens.

Tamar trails

❯ TAMAR VALLEY, DEVON

How to get there:

To try out the tracks for yourself you need to be a member of the Woodland Riders group or buy a day pass. The Woodlands and Gawton tracks are just off the B3257.
Nearest railway station: Bere Alston (3 miles)
There is no bus service.

Find out more:

www.woodlandriders.com
01822 618 178

Other things to see:

If you'd rather take to the Tamar Valley on two feet rather than two wheels there are free AONB trail guides to help you explore the area's mining history while protecting its vital habitats. They can be downloaded from www.tamarvalley.org.uk.

The Prince of Wales Mine and Engine House near Minions, overlooking the Tamar Valley. Along with the Tamar Valley mines, it is part of the Cornwall and West Devon Mining Landscape World Heritage Site.

It's easy to see why the Tamar Valley is so popular with mountain bikers. The area around the 50-mile long River Tamar, which separates Devon from Cornwall, was a mining hotspot for nearly a thousand years. Tin, silver, granite, copper and lead were extracted from the earth and the network of old mine chimneys, hidden quays and lunar-like spoil-tips is just too tempting for mountain bikers. But it wasn't always the safe day out it now is.

The industrial past that earned the valley World Heritage Site status in 2006 also left it with a more deadly legacy. As demand for tin and copper began to flag, a by-product of the extraction process took centre stage and kept the mines in production long after they could have faced closure. Where there was copper, there was arsenic and by the 1870s the mines alongside the Tamar were producing over half the world's supply of the poison.

While the last mines closed in the early 20th century, what remained was a large number of arsenic-contaminated areas which modern-day mountain bikers were unintentionally disturbing. The arsenic could be inhaled from the dirt kicked up on a rigorous ride or enter the bloodstream via cuts and grazes. Apart from the danger to the thrill-seekers themselves, there were concerns that their bikes would inadvertently spread the poison to clean areas and potentially destabilize previously safe heaps from which arsenic could run into the river and hence into the water supply of the city of Plymouth.

There was a further environmental problem. Not only were the bikers spreading arsenic around, putting the delicate ecosystem under threat, they were completely unaware of the vital habitats they were crashing through. The Tamar Valley is a Site of Special Scientific Interest, home to nightjars, endangered lichen and the incredibly rare heath fritillary butterflies. The last thing that the Tamar Valley Area of Outstanding Natural Beauty wanted was to discourage mountain bikers from coming to the region so, working with the Earl of Byford and the Tavistock Woodland Estate, the organization secured £7 million of funding to build trails to provide public access to the mining landscape and construct safe new tracks for bikers. You can now enjoy this beautiful landscape free from danger to yourself, others and the environment.

Three trails have been opened in Maddacleave Woods near the old Gawton Mine. These are graded according to level of expertise from the death-defying Super-Tavi and Egypt – both of which require a daredevil mentality and body-armour – to the easier HSD (High Speed Descent) track. Still, with sections that drop off 500 feet in just one mile, adrenalin-inducing jumps and nerve-shredding bends, this is an exhilarating way to experience a spectacular slice of industrial heritage.

Pure Dartmoor

❯ DARTMOOR, DEVON

Every year 2.5 million visitors descend on the wilds of Dartmoor to experience this rugged, sometimes unforgiving expanse. The stark moorland covers an area of 400 square miles, dotted with tors, the rocky outcrops that formed some 280 million years ago as the granite that makes up most of the landscape cooled down. It's a land steeped in legend and mystery, full of ceremonial cromlechs and ancient tombs.

Dartmoor was also one of the first National Parks, created in 1951. When it received its designation there was only one real choice for its logo, a symbol that for millions represents this brooding but strangely compelling landscape: the hardy Dartmoor pony.

There is archaeological evidence that domesticated ponies grazed the moorland 3,500 years ago, helping to maintain this important habitat, and for centuries served the locals well, pulling carts and carrying loads. Yet today, pureblood Dartmoor ponies – those with a known pedigree – are an endangered species, believed to be rarer than the Giant Panda.

When the National Park was created, some 30,000 ponies roamed Dartmoor. The closure of the mines and quarries has meant that their usefulness as a packhorse has been all but lost and today their numbers are estimated to be nearer 3,000. Of those, only around 500 native purebloods survive, outnumbered by the introduced Shetlands and by Arab and Thoroughbred crossbreeds.

The ponies live in small herds on the moor all year round, foaling between May and August. Then in September and October the pony drifts, the annual round-ups, are held. The ponies are herded off the moors where they are separated into groups according to owner. They are checked out, treated if necessary and some are sent to market. The remainder are returned to the moor, with any new foals branded to indicate their owner. Unlike the purebloods, which are too valuable to roam freely on the moor, the price of a standard pony has plummeted – a Dartmoor pony now struggles to fetch £10 at market. This devaluation threatens one of the oldest traditions on Dartmoor.

But all is not lost. The Park authority has acknowledged the importance of saving their own symbol and have begun to offer subsidies for the upkeep of pony herds or to expand their use for conservation grazing.

How to get there:
Take the A38 to Plymouth, turning off at Bovey Tracey. The High Moorland Visitor Centre at Princetown on the B3212 is a great place to start.
For sat nav users: PL20 6QF
Nearest railway stations: Exeter, Newton Abbot, Totnes, Ivybridge and Plymouth.
Bus services:
www.traveline.org.uk/index.htm
0871 200 22 33

Find out more:
www.dartmoor.co.uk
01837 52200

Other things to see:
Castle Drogo at Drewsteignton was the last castle to be built in England.
For sat nav users: EX6 6PB
www.nationaltrust.org.uk/castledrogo
01647 433 306

Ponies grazing beside Chinkwell Tor, Dartmoor.

John Craven's ideal island ❯❯

I love a good island and Lundy, about 11 miles off the coast of north Devon, is definitely that. There's only a small landing area and so in bad weather arriving by boat can be a bit dodgy, but it's worth the effort. The waters around the island, designated Britain's first Marine Conservation Zone in January 2010, are teeming with life from grey seals and lobsters to a fantastic variety of coral.

The island is only 3 miles long so it's easy to get to see all its attractions, from the lighthouse to the Marisco Tavern, the only pub on Lundy. You have to be careful to time your visit to the gent's loo at the pub, especially in bad weather: there's no roof but you're treated to a great view! I actually filmed that for *Countryfile* – from a discreet camera angle of course!

Silver darlings

> ## CLOVELLY, DEVON

When the summer season is in full swing, it's hard to believe that scarcely a soul knew this beautiful cliff-top village even existed before the mid-19th century. In *A Message from the Sea* (1860) Charles Dickens renamed the village Steepways, but it was Charles Kingsley, author of *The Water Babies*, who put the place on the map with his 1855 novel *Westward Ho!*. Kingsley had lived here as a child between 1831 and 1836 when his father served first as Senior Curate and then Rector.

While things have changed from Kingsley's day, Clovelly has stubbornly refused to keep pace, giving you the chance to step back in time. And step you must if you want to visit. The single cobbled street linking the village with its tiny working harbour falls 400 feet in just half a mile, making it a haven from wheeled transport. Instead, heavy deliveries are made by sled and occasionally by the donkeys you regularly see trotting between the delightful cob houses.

Clovelly's unique charm survives because it has been owned by the same family since 1738. Private ownership has ensured that second-home owners have been kept to a minimum and only two hotels offer bed and board. Of course, the village's buzzing atmosphere, full of artistry and truly cottage industry, now attracts many tourists and its steeply sloping street is packed in summer.

Clovelly hasn't always relied on tourism. Until the mid-20th century a thriving herring trade kept the villagers employed. When Kingsley was a boy over 100 boats were based at the port, landing 9,000 herrings on a single good catch. To this day, the locals swear by what they call their 'silver darlings'. While the herring may have fallen out of favour after the Second World War, ports such as Clovelly are striving to help them swim back on to our dinner plates. Every autumn the village holds a herring festival celebrating the silver darlings, alongside shanty drinking, a smattering of maritime history and lashings of cider.

How to get there:

Exit the M5 at Junction 27. Head west on the A39 from Bideford and take the B3237 to Clovelly. Disabled access is limited, owing to the steep cobbled High Street but a fare-paying Land-Rover service operates Easter–Oct from the Visitor Centre.

For sat nav users: EX39 5TA

Nearest railway station: Barnstaple (16 miles)

Bus services: www.cornwallpublictransport. info

0871 200 22 33

Find out more:

www.clovelly.co.uk

01237 431 781

A donkey used for deliveries at Clovelly (above); the main, cobbled street running down to the sea (right).

Other things to see:
Crazy Kate's is the oldest cottage in Clovelly, boasting the best views across the harbour. It is named after a poor fisherman's wife who sat watching from the cottage as her husband was drowned in a storm. Driven mad with grief she put on her wedding dress and ran to join him beneath the waves.

Clovelly harbour front showing Crazy Kate's Cottage (centre) at the edge of the beach.

The excited giant
❯ CERNE ABBAS, DORSET

Cerne Abbas is a vibrant and historic community, which in the last few years was named Britain's most desirable village. However, its most notable feature largely overshadows its charms: a 55-metre naked giant carved into the hillside complete with knobbled club and an 8-metre long erect penis. Although the age of the giant is a topic of debate – John Hutchin's 1774 *History of Dorset* claims it to be a 'modern thing', cut out between 1641 and 1666 – the supposed fertility symbol has been subjected to many publicity stunts. Over time he has been given a wife and even a neighbour in the form of a gigantic Homer Simpson playing hoopla with a doughnut.

Whatever his origins, the excited giant needs a gang of National Trust volunteers to restore his uncompromising looks every seven years. The top layer of chalk is removed, taking with it the algae, lichen and weeds that creep over the giant's lines. This is recycled, used to fill in pot-holes in local roads, while new chalk is packed into its place and sealed with water. The slope itself is too steep for the grass to be cut by machine so a flock of sheep is brought in twice a year to graze away, oblivious to the shocking image beneath their feet.

How to get there:
The 'Rude Giant' is found ½ mile north of Cerne Abbas. The best viewpoint is beside the A352. Nearest railway station: Maiden Newton (4 miles) Bus services: www.traveline.org.uk 0871 200 22 33

Find out more:
www.cerneabbas.org 01237 431 781

Other things to see:
St Augustine's Well, supposed to be blessed by the saint himself, is found near Abbey Street in Cerne Abbas. It is said that if you look into the well on Easter morning you will see, staring back at you, the faces of those who will die in the year ahead.

The Cerne Abbas Giant needs help maintaining its handsome looks, including the help of some hungry sheep (overleaf).

Far from the madding crowd
❯ HARDY'S COTTAGE AND MAX GATE, DORSET

Hardy's Cottage, birthplace of the novelist and poet.

Thomas Hardy is forever linked to Dorset, the county he immortalised as his fictional Wessex. The author was born in 1840 at Hardy's Cottage near Dorchester, the family home constructed in 1800 by his great-grandfather, John Hardy, a traditional builder. The walls are built of cob – a mixture of local gravel, chalk, clay, sand, flint and straw – although in later years they were faced with brick to protect them against the elements. Hardy lived here until moving to London to train as an architect in 1860, although he regularly returned to his family home to write *Under the Greenwood Tree* (1872) and *Far from the Madding Crowd* (1874).

Hardy wrote in a small room upstairs in the cottage from where he would have been able to see the Hardy Monument on Black Down, erected to commemorate a distant relative, Vice-Admiral Sir Thomas Masterman Hardy, famous for being asked to pucker up by a dying Nelson. Hardy loved this cottage. Even after it was rented out following his parents' death he would pop round to give the tenants tips on its maintenance. How pleased he would be that the visitors who make the pilgrimage here every summer still find it much as it was described in *Under the Greenwood Tree*: 'a long low cottage with a hipped roof of thatch and three chimneys'.

The peaceful country garden is also exactly as he would have remembered it, packed with lavender, marigolds, lilies and lupins, and, behind the cottage, his beloved Puddletown Forest is much the same today too, save for the conifers planted by the Forestry Commission after the Second World War. This tranquil mixed woodland was transformed in *The Return of the Native* (1878) into the gateway to the bleak, rabbit-scratched Egdon Heath. Every year without fail, Hardy used to return to Puddletown Forest on his birthday for a ramble beneath the chestnut, hazel, ash and birch trees.

Later in life Hardy remained close to his place of birth. Max Gate, a modest villa, was designed by Hardy himself and built in 1885 by his father and brother on a plot purchased from the Duchy of Cornwall. Originally he feared that its building might bankrupt him, but the success of *Jude the Obscure* (1895) put plenty of money in the Hardy coffers. It was at Max Gate that Hardy wrote *The Mayor of Casterbridge* (1886) and *Tess of the d'Urbervilles* (1891), and it remained his home until his death in 1928. Unfortunately his time here was less idyllic than his childhood at Hardy's Cottage. His marriage to his first wife, Emma, was an unhappy one although Hardy only realized just how much pain he had caused her when, after her death in 1912, he discovered her journal. It was simply entitled 'What I think of my husband'. Whatever their relationship, Hardy's heart is buried with Emma at Stinsford Parish Church. The quiet churchyard had been the author's preferred last resting place but when the executor of his will, Sir Sydney Carlyle Cockerell, insisted that his remains be interred in Poets' Corner at Westminster Abbey a compromise was found. His ashes were sent to London while his heart, appropriately, was laid to rest in his beloved Dorset.

How to get there:
Hardy's Cottage, now owned by the National Trust, is situated in Higher Bockhampton, just off the A35 north east of Dorchester. It is open Sun–Thurs from mid-Mar–Oct. Max Gate, also owned by the National Trust, can be found on the A352, a mile east of Dorchester. The hall, dining and drawing rooms are open Apr–Sept on Mon, Wed and Sun. For sat nav users: DT2 8QJ
Nearest railway station: Dorchester (4 miles from Hardy's Cottage, 1 mile from Max Gate)
Bus services:
www.coachhousetravel.co.uk
01305 267 644

Find out more:
www.nationaltrust.org.uk/hardyscottage
01305 262 366

Other things to see:
Hardy's study from Max Gate has been reconstructed at the Dorset County Museum in Dorchester. The room is presented almost exactly how it was left on the day he died and contains many of Hardy's own first editions of his books and the pens he used.
For sat nav users: DT1 1XA
www.dorsetcountymuseum.org
01305 262 735

Thomas Hardy's body may be buried in Westminster Abbey, but his heart lies in Dorset.

A challenge with a sting

❭ MARSHWOOD, DORSET

How to get there:

The Bottle Inn is at Marshwood
near Bridport on the A3066.
For sat nav users: DT6 5QJ
Nearest railway station:
Axminster (5 miles)
Bus services:
www.traveline.org.uk
0871 200 22 33

Find out more:

www.thebottleinn.co.uk
01297 678 254

Contestants tuck in
at the annual World
Stinging Nettle Eating
Championships.

One of Britain's most bizarre new traditions started with an argument in a pub. In 1986, two local farmers were bickering over who had the longest stinging nettles on their land. The landlady of the Bottle Inn decided the only way to settle the argument was to have a competition to find the longest nettles in the county. Three years later, the longest-nettle competition took a surprising twist. Alex Williams, a local hospital porter and ex-guardsman, entered a nettle over 4.5 metres long, saying 'If anyone beats that, I'll eat it.' Unfortunately for Alex an American couple holidaying nearby produced a 4.8 metre nettle and, true to his word, he wolfed down his losing stinger. The act made Alex a local celebrity and over time the challenge was set to see if anyone could stomach more nettles than him. The World Stinging Nettle Eating Championships were born.

Every year over 70 contestants take to the stage to munch through as many nettles as possible. The rules are simple. You have one hour to feast and all leaves from each stem must be eaten for the length to count.

It can be a painful experience for the contestants. Nettles have a thin layer of hollow hairs much like hypodermic needles. When the hairs brush against your skin, they break off, piercing the flesh to inject formic acid. Thankfully, as countrymen have known for centuries, mother nature provides a handy remedy. The alkaline found in burdock leaves or moss neutralises the nettle's acid if rubbed on the affected area. Not that the nettle-eating contestants have such relief to hand. The trick from the champions is to roll the leaf inwards to cover as many of the tiny needles as possible then swallow as quickly as you can.

Over the years *Countryfile* has sent two of its fearless reporters to rise to Alex's challenge. In 2002 Ben Fogle was left with a black tongue after eating 6.7 metres of nettles, while, in 2009, ethno-botanist James Wong managed 10 metres. Sadly for James some of his stems were disqualified as he'd left on the odd leaf.

Other things to see:
Chesil Beach is an 18-mile long shingle spit stretching north west from Portland to West Bay. Separated at points from the mainland by the Fleet Lagoon, it is said that in days past sailors used to tell their location by the size of the stones: they are pebble sized at Abbotsbury but can be 15 centimetres wide at Portland.

Chesil Beach from the air.

Plain survival

▶ SALISBURY PLAIN, WILTSHIRE

How to get there:

Private tours can be arranged to the Great Bustard site. Directions are given when you contact the UK Great Bustard Group on 07817 971 327. The conservation groups involved try not to advertise the exact location to avoid undue disturbance for the birds.

Find out more:

www.greatbustard.com

07817 971 327

Salisbury Plain, a 40,468-hectare (100,000-acre) area of chalk upland just north of Salisbury, is largely owned by the Ministry of Defence and has been used since the 19th century for firing ranges and tank manoeuvres. Despite these activities, there are a surprising number of public footpaths that remain open even during exercises. This unique environment has proved extremely beneficial for one rather special bird, the Great Bustard. It is a stunning creature, similar in shape to a goose, standing 1.2 metres tall and weighing up to 13.5kg and boasting a beautiful plumage of blue-grey feathers around the head and neck with a black and brown body and tail.

In the early 19th century the Great Bustard was described as 'the largest, noblest and most highly prized of all our British birds'. Unfortunately, even as those words were written the birds' habitat was being eroded by changes in agriculture and by the 1840s they had been hunted to extinction in Britain by both fox and man. Their plight has been mirrored around the world with the global population estimated to be just 35,000 individuals.

In 2004, a programme began to reintroduce them to Salisbury Plain. The chalk grassland is an ideal habitat for this particularly shy breed, because the military presence has kept the Plain pretty much as it has been for centuries, untouched by enclosure acts or modern agriculture. In the first year 22 chicks were transported from Russia to Wiltshire and since then a further four batches have arrived. Of the 80 chicks brought to Britain, 16 have survived, a success rate of 20 per cent, but in recent years there have been more exciting developments.

July 2007 saw the first Great Bustard egg laid on British soil since 1832, a massive boost to the reintroduction project. Although the first discovery was found not to have been fertilised, two years later the first chicks were hatched in England. One died but the other survived in a nest site that was understandably kept secret. How cheering to know that in this small part of the world the birds are able to live in peace for the first time in their history.

Guided tours of the Great Bustard's range are available, although visitors to the area may be lucky enough to spot the world's heaviest flying birds unaided as they do sometimes wander. Amazingly, the birds seem unperturbed by vehicles on the plain, even army manoeuvres, but are wary of humans and can become agitated if people approach within a kilometre of them. A good pair of binoculars is a must and it's best not to leave your car if you see one.

Other things to see:
Stonehenge is just a five-minute drive from the Great Bustard site, at the junction of the A344 and A303 where there is parking and a visitor centre. (There are plans to close the section of the A344 closest to the monument and build a new visitor centre by 2012.) Although you can't walk into the ring itself there are leaflets available that guide you on trails around the World Heritage Site. The famous ring is only part of a whole complex of ancient monuments.

The prehistoric stone circle of Stonehenge.

Britain's smallest parish church

❭ CULBONE, SOMERSET

Britain's famous beauty spots and sites of historic or scientific interest are well-advertised and signposted. However, as always in the British countryside, if you wander away from the usual roads and footpaths, hidden gems are waiting to be discovered. Such a place is Culbone. Lying two miles from the nearest regular road and on a track that no car, except the odd 4x4 should attempt, it's nestled at the bottom of the Culbone Valley, the walls of which tower some 365 metres above you.

People make this pilgrimage to visit Culbone's church, Britain's smallest parish church in regular use. You can't really even call Culbone a village – even hamlet stretches the point – as apart from two houses, the part-Saxon church is the only building in the valley. It has stood in this valley for nearly 800 years and can accommodate 33 people in its 3.6-metre wide nave. The entire building is only a mere 10.6 metres in length. Lit by candle – no electricity here – it's easy to forget that this isn't a relic of the past but a living place of worship. Granted, the congregation may only comprise six people most Sundays, but come Christmas or harvest festival, the pews are packed and it's a popular location for weddings. Imagine your guests having to walk all that way to witness your vows!

How to get there:
Turn off the A39 opposite the Culbone Stables Inn and drive down the narrow path, parking as near to where it crosses Yearnor Mill Lane. Then prepare yourself for a steep 1½-mile hike through the wood. And don't forget, you've got to walk back up afterwards!
For sat nav users: TA24 8AA
Nearest railway station: Minehead (11.5 miles)
There is no bus service.

Find out more:
www.exmoor-nationalpark.
gov.uk
01398 323 665

Culbone feels remote by today's standard so you can't help but wonder how cut off it must have been in days gone by. When the church's corner stones were originally laid, the surrounding oaks and walnut trees would have supplied timber for Porlock's docks. However, after the settlement served briefly as a camp for French prisoners of war in the 14th century, Culbone was established as a leper colony in 1544, a role it played for 78 years. Search around its walls and you'll find a hagioscope, or leper's window, which allowed the afflicted to watch the Eucharist without coming in contact with the congregation.

Over 460 years later, Culbone is a bewitching refuge, hidden away from the bustle and crowds of 21st-century life.

Other things to see:
No visit to this corner of Exmoor is complete without a trip to Porlock Weir, once a busy port and now a picturesque harbour situated on the South West Coast Path. If you're feeling energetic, you could pick up the Coast Path in Porlock and visit Culbone en route to Lynmouth.
For sat nav users: TA24 8PB

The remote, pretty parish church of Culbone.

The Rock of Ages

❯ BURRINGTON COMBE GORGE, SOMERSET

A flash of lightning was the first warning the young cleric had that the storm was approaching. As thunder rumbled over Burrington Combe Gorge, he pulled his coat around him, aware that as soon as the rain lashed in he would be wet to the skin. When the skies opened, Augustus Montague Toplady, curate of nearby Blagdon, rushed for a narrow cleft in the sheer rockface beside him and took refuge. As he watched the tempest, safe and dry, words came to him, a song of praise inspired by his temporary haven. With no paper in his pockets, he feared that he would forget his composition on his return journey. Glancing down, he saw a discarded playing card at his feet and, praying that the Almighty would forgive him for using such a sinful object, he snatched it up and wrote the first couple of lines:

> *Rock of Ages, cleft for me,*
> *let me hide myself in Thee.*

No one really knows how much truth there is in the local tale of Toplady and the Rock of Ages; the cleft is suspiciously narrow and you do wonder how much shelter it would offer the black and red six-spot burnet moths that frequent the area, let alone a 19th-century reverend, but thousands of people visit the spot every year. Few could be disappointed by the stupendous cliffs themselves. Burrington Combe Gorge, while not on the grand scale of nearby Cheddar, is a superb example of a typical Mendips limestone gorge. In places the cliff face is a staggering 76 metres high.

The Rock of Ages is also a great starting point for a stroll across Black Down. The view from Beacon Batch, the highest point of the Mendip Hills at 325 metres, is spectacular, taking in the towers of the two Severn bridges and Brean Down.

There are several Bronze Age round barrows found around Beacon Batch but in more recent times another settlement was built. During the Second World War, a decoy town was constructed in the hope that its lights would distract German bombers from targeting Bristol. As you walk keep a lookout for mounds of earth laid out in vertical lines. Each of these would have had a beacon on top to simulate the lights of windows.

How to get there:
From Bristol, take the A38 towards Bristol International Airport. Four miles past the airport follow signs for Burrington.
Nearest railway station:
Yatton (7 miles)
Bus services:
www.firstgroup.com
0845 602 0156

Find out more
www.mendip.gov.uk/visiting
01749 648 999

Other things to see:
England's smallest city is Wells, named after the number of natural wells that spring here. It has been the seat of the Bishop of Bath and Wells since 1206. The Bishop's palace is one of the most fortified in Britain with its own drawbridge, portcullis and moat. Wells Cathedral, a Gothic masterpiece, is also home to the Quarter Jack, one of the very earliest mechanical clocks in the country.
For sat nav users: BA5 2US
www.wellscathedral.org.uk
01749 674 483

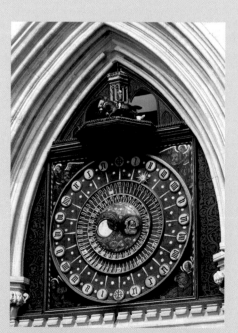

Quarter Jack, the elaborate mechanical clock at Wells Cathedral.

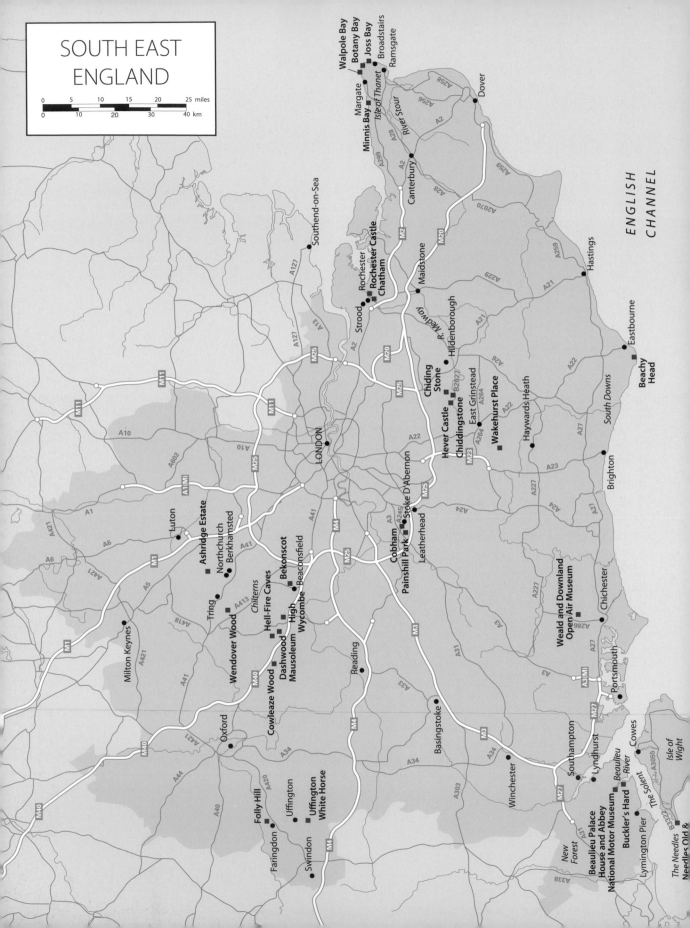

SOUTH EAST ENGLAND

0   5   10   15   20   25 miles
0   10   20   30   40 km

Walpole Bay
Botany Bay
Joss Bay
Broadstairs
Ramsgate
Margate
Minnis Bay
Isle of Thanet
River Stour
Dover
ENGLISH CHANNEL
Canterbury

Southend-on-Sea

Rochester
Rochester Castle
Chatham
Strood
Maidstone
Medway R.
Hildenborough
Hastings

Chiding Stone
Chiddingstone
East Grinstead
Wakehurst Place
Haywards Heath
Eastbourne
Beachy Head

Hever Castle
South Downs
Brighton

LONDON

Stoke D'Abernon
Cobham
Painshill Park
Leatherhead

Luton
Ashridge Estate
Northchurch
Berkhamsted
Tring

Chilterns
Bekonscot
Beaconsfield
Hell-Fire Caves
High Wycombe
Wendover Wood
Dashwood Mausoleum
Cowleaze Wood

Milton Keynes

Chichester
Weald and Downland Open Air Museum
Portsmouth

Reading
Basingstoke
Winchester
Southampton
Lyndhurst

Oxford

Folly Hill
Uffington
Uffington White Horse
Faringdon
Swindon

New Forest
Beaulieu Palace House and Abbey
National Motor Museum
Buckler's Hard
Lymington Pier
The Solent
Beaulieu River
Cowes
Isle of Wight
The Needles
Needles Old &

South East

Fed up with sitting in that gridlock in the centre of the capital? Need to breathe fresh air rather than car fumes and the odours drifting from the nearest fast-food joint? Then you're in luck, because London has a wealth of glorious countryside right on its doorstep.

Whether you're travelling from central London or further afield the South East has many treasures to explore. There's the ancient woodland of the Chiltern Hills, the unchanged commons of the New Forest and the beautiful beaches of the Isle of Thanet. History comes alive at the former port of Buckler's Hard and the Weald and Downland Open Air Museum, while the present is preserved for the future in the vaults of Kew's Millennium Seed Bank.

Surprises also await, with relics of the time when Britain stood neck and neck with the United States and USSR in the Space Race, and built the coal-powered pleasure cruisers, one of which still steams down the rivers of Kent. There really is no excuse for not getting out there to explore.

The time-warp garden

❯ PAINSHILL PARK, SURREY

Dockey Wood,
Hertfordshire (previous
page); the Gothic folly
seen across a frozen lake
at Painshill Park (below).

In 1974, Norman Kitz, who lived near Painshill Park Lake in Surrey, took a walk and made a startling discovery. In an overgrown corner of the park he found what appeared to be an ancient ruined abbey. Lost amidst the wilderness of a once-glorious garden, the abbey, built by the lake so that it was reflected in the water, had remained, untouched for nearly two hundred years, hidden from sight and forgotten by the world.

In fact this beautiful spot never boasted its own ecclesiastical house. The abbey was built in 1772, designed as a ruin, a folly from day one by a man who was to change the face of English gardens for ever.

Visitors to Painshill Park could be forgiven for thinking that they have stepped into a perfectly natural environment but, like the ruined abbey, the entire estate was carefully manufactured. It was the brainchild of Charles Hamilton, the youngest son of the Earl of Abercorn. On returning from a grand tour of Europe, Hamilton was seized by the desire to create the ultimate pleasure garden and in 1738 purchased a barren, unproductive heath. For 35 years Hamilton worked this barren soil. Looking beyond the formal and herbal gardens of the time, he imported exotic shrubs, trees and plants from North America, using the services of botanist John Bartram and his business partner Peter Collinson. Bartram collected plants from the colonies and shipped them overseas to Collinson who distributed them to various horticulturists and garden designers, including Hamilton. The journey across the Atlantic, taking anything from five weeks to three months, was fraught with difficulties. If a box of seeds survived being destroyed by salt or eaten by rats, it could demand five guineas in the English market – around £500 in today's prices.

Hamilton's first seeds from Collinson arrived in 1748 and formed the basis of his garden. Rejecting the formal lines of traditional gardens, Hamilton attempted to create landscapes, studded with impressive follies and structures, that would inspire the heart. It was the first time an English garden had bloomed with sunflowers, Michaelmas daisies and magnolia, while new shrubs provided swatches of red leaves in autumn, a splash of warmth at a time when English gardens were devoid of colour.

Hamilton's dream ended in 1773 when, near bankrupt, he was forced to sell the gardens. Over the years the estate went through a succession of owners, none of whom held on to it long enough to modernise the grounds in the new Victorian style that dominated most grand gardens. By the time the abbey was rediscovered in the 1970s the park had been split up and largely abandoned, its treasures lost beneath creeping weeds. Today, thanks to the work of the Park's trust, it has been returned to its 18th-century glory, the follies rebuilt and the gardens replanted in line with Hamilton's stunning vision.

How to get there:
Painshill Park, located on the A245 between Cobham and Leatherhead, is open daily.
For sat nav users: KT11 1JE
Nearest railway station: Cobham & Stoke D'Abernon (1½ miles)
Bus services: www.travelinesoutheast.org.uk
0871 200 2233

Find out more:
www.painshill.co.uk
01932 868 113

Other things to see:
Surrey's only working watermill is found in nearby Cobham. Restored by a volunteer team in the 1990s, Cobham Mill is open every second Sunday afternoon, Apr–Oct.
For sat nav users: KT11 3AL
www.cobhamheritage.org.uk
01932 867 387

Julia Bradbury tastes gourmet garlic on the Isle of Wight »

The Isle of Wight is synonymous with sailing and sure enough on our visit I found myself experiencing Cowes Week, the longest-running and biggest sailing regatta of its kind.

But my overriding memory of the Isle is biting into a chunk of 'Purple Heritage' Moldovan garlic. Never have I popped something so strong-tasting in to my mouth. Imagine the most powerful onion you can find, times it by 500 and throw in some scorching chillies. I literally jolted with the taste. The cameraman loved it.

Once I had recovered, exploring the UK's largest garlic farm was fascinating. The owner, Colin Boswell, thinks that the quality of light on the island is perfect for cultivating this pongy treat and he should know as he travels the world looking for the best garlic possible. The sheer number of garlic varieties on the Isle of Wight is staggering, from the stuff you're used to seeing in the supermarket to the ginormous Elephant Garlic, which is the size of a globe artichoke. Apparently, those in the know deny it's true garlic, claiming that it's nearer an oversized spring onion. It certainly smelt like garlic to me.

Britain's space race
› THE NEEDLES, ISLE OF WIGHT

How to get there:

High Down (also called the Needles New Battery) is found at the end of the B3322 but there is no vehicular access (best to take a Needles Tour Bus). Open weekends only, Mar–Nov (11am–3pm), but closed in high winds. Disabled access by arrangement.
For sat nav users: PO39 0JH
Nearest railway stations: Lymington Pier and Portsmouth Harbour (linked to Isle of Wight by ferry, hovercraft and catamaran)
Bus services:
www.islandbuses.info
0871 200 2233

When you visit the windswept headland above the world-famous Needles at the western tip of the Isle of Wight, it's hard to believe that just over thirty years ago this remote spot was the hub for Britain's very own space programme.

In the 1960s, Britain was neck-and-neck with America and the USSR in the Space Race. On 3 October 1952 Britain detonated its first nuclear bomb. The next task was to develop the perfect inter-continental missile to deliver such a devastating weapon and the search for a test site began.

West High Down, above the Needles, fitted the bill perfectly. Topographically it was a natural bowl, which meant the noise of any explosions would be projected out to sea and away from populated areas. The site is also riddled with subterranean tunnels in the chalk owing to its former use as a lookout post against the threat of Napoleonic invasion. In 1957, the test site opened.

Missiles, codenamed Black Knights, were constructed in Cowes and transported to High Down for testing. Once safely anchored to the ground, the rockets were put through their paces before being shipped over to Woomera in South Australia for launching.

Over 200 people worked on the site, which was supposed to be highly classified, but as the range was guarded by soldiers wearing uniforms emblazoned with 'Rocket Development Dept' and the missiles were trundled out in massive containers with the legend 'Rock Ran Woomera' down the side (the name Woomera was synonymous with the testing of long-range missiles), the true nature of the work at High Down was a rather open secret.

Between 1958 and 1965, 23 Black Knight missiles were launched before Britain's nuclear programme slowed down and the scientists at High Down turned their attention to outer space. On a shoestring budget, work began on the Black Arrow project and, in 1971, after several test runs, *Prospero*, the first – and to date the last – all-British satellite went into orbit.

Success was short-lived because the government, faced with a financial downturn, abandoned its space programme to concentrate on a project it was to develop with France – Concorde. The only visible evidence that the United Kingdom came so close to conquering the final frontier is a scattering of concrete structures in this corner of southern England. Yet, high above your head, the ultimate tribute to the pioneering work of the High Down scientists still soars; *Prospero* continues its orbit of the Earth three decades after its launch.

The Needles with the Old and New Batteries perched precariously on the familiar white cliffs.

Other things to see:

On a separate site next to the remains of High Downs test site is the Old Battery. Built in 1862 to protect Britain from French invasion, the fort has original Victorian gun barrels on display and fantastic views of the Needles. The Needles formation took its name from the 36-metre high needle-shaped rock known as Lot's Wife. Sadly, the structure was as doomed as its biblical namesake when it collapsed into the sea in 1764. At the end of the landmark you'll see the 33-metre high lighthouse, opened in 1859, which replaced the original because it was positioned too high above sea level to be any use in a storm.

Find out more:

www.nationaltrust.org.uk/main/
w-theneedlesoldbattery
01983 754 772

Little Britain

▶ BEKONSCOT MODEL VILLAGE, BUCKINGHAMSHIRE

How to get there:

Follow the brown tourist signs
for Bekonscot from the A40 to
Beaconsfield Old Town.

For sat nav users: HP9 2PL

Nearest railway station:
Beaconsfield (under ½ mile)

Bus services:

www.travelinesoutheast.org.uk

0870 608 268

Find out more:

www.bekonscot.co.uk

01494 672 919

There is a small corner of England where the local shops have withstood the relentless march of modern supermarkets, where post offices remain open and the trains are never late. Unfortunately, unless you're 10 centimetres tall and carved from wood you've no chance of being welcomed into this idyllic community.

Bekonscot is said to be the world's oldest model village. Within its 0.6 hectares (1.5 acres) you can find 200 buildings, occupied by more than 3,000 tiny inhabitants and 1,000 animals. You'll also discover some of the worst puns known to man. Only in Bekonscot can you buy bread from a baker called Ivan Huvan, call on the services of plumber Lee Key or instruct the solicitors of Argue & Twist to represent you in your lawsuit against greengrocer Chris P. Lettis.

The six miniature towns that make up Bekonscot were created by a wealthy accountant, Roland Callingham, in the 1920s. When his model railway threatened to take over their home, the long-suffering Mrs Callingham gave her husband an ultimatum: either the trains went or she did. Luckily for their marriage, Callingham bought a neighbouring meadow and began creating a rural landscape for his specially commissioned 1:32 scale Gauge 1 railway. Assisted by his housekeeper, chauffeur and gardener, Callingham soon started to add miniature buildings, and transformed his swimming pool into the village lake.

Initially, Callingham had no intention of opening his toy kingdom to the public, but news of its Lilliputian pleasures started to spread. Encouraged by friends and family he opened its doors in August 1929 and in 1934, Queen Mary even brought princesses Elizabeth and Margaret to celebrate her eldest granddaughter's eighth birthday.

At first, time didn't stand still and as the outside world changed, so did the tiny realm of Bekonscot. The aerodrome of the 1950s proudly boasted new-fangled jet planes and diesel trains roared around the track. However, the Church Army, who took over running of the attraction in 1976, made the decision in the 1990s to turn back the clock. The towns and their occupants were carefully remodelled to return Bekonscot to the countryside of the 1930s, where it has remained frozen in time ever since. At least one new building, which takes three months to build, is added every year and each figure, now moulded in resin, is repainted every 12 months.

Amazingly, Bekonscot still manages to weave its magic in an age of high-octane theme parks, a testament to the child-like eccentricity of its founder and our constant need for nostalgia. While the only white-knuckle rides you'll find are those enjoyed by the model villagers themselves in their fun fair, the biggest smallest attraction remains the miniature railway: 450 metres of track is controlled from a full-size, computerised level-frame signal box donated by the town of Purley in Surrey in the 1980s.

Other things to see:

Nearby High Wycombe with its lovely Georgian Little Market House is well worth a wander. The town has a peculiar custom where, during the annual mayoral elections in May, they publicly weigh their outgoing mayor on a huge set of scales to ensure that he hasn't been getting fat at the taxpayer's expense over the past year.

For sat nav users: HP11 2XE

www.visitbuckinghamshire.org

The quaint, miniature village of Bekonscot.

Matt Baker's bird's-eye view of the Chilterns »

Leaving the open Durham Dales for London to start work on *Blue Peter* was one of the most difficult decisions I've ever made. I'd never felt the pull of the Big Smoke, so it's no wonder that I soon settled in the middle of the beautiful Chiltern Hills. It truly is a wonderful part of the world.

I got to see it in a different light when we visited the hills to celebrate the twentieth anniversary of the red kite's reintroduction to the area. I received my own kite's-eye view as a passenger on a fixed-wing glider, courtesy of the Royal Air Force Gliding and Soaring Association. The military use gliding as a way of relaxing service men and women who have returned from stressful postings such as Iraq and Afghanistan. Relaxing wasn't the word I would use. As this was my first time in a fixed-wing glider my pilot decided to pull some extreme aerobatic manoeuvres. It isn't easy delivering a piece-to-camera when your stomach has just been somewhere around your ears!

How to get there:

The Ashridge Estate is a good place from which to explore the Chilterns. It is located 3 miles north of the A41, off the B4506 from Northchurch.
For sat nav users: HP4 1LT
Nearest railway station:
Tring (7 miles)
Bus services:
www.arrivabus.co.uk
0871 200 22 33

Find out more:

www.chilternsaonb.org
01844 355 500

Other things to see:

At the summit of West Wycombe Hill is the Dashwood Mausoleum, built in 1765. Beneath its majestic flint columns lurk the Hell-Fire Caves.
www.hellfirecaves.co.uk
01494 533 739

A carpet of bluebells in Dockey Wood, on the Ashridge Estate.

Bluebell country

❯ CHILTERNS

Oxfordshire, Berkshire, Buckinghamshire, Hertfordshire and Bedfordshire

In January, when most plants are still sheltering beneath the earth, the first shoots of bluebells appear. Starting early to get in as much growth as possible before the leaves of the trees shade the woodland floor, the stage is set for the millions of *Hyacinthoides* that bloom between April and June. Britain's bluebell displays are world famous – in fact half of the planet's entire bluebell population is said to be contained within our woods – and there's no better place to marvel at the carpets of blue and white than the Chilterns.

Just a short hop from London, the Chilterns form a graceful 40-mile arc of green and chalk hills. The 'Domesday Book' marked the area as the second-most wooded region of England in AD 1086 and even today nearly 25 per cent of the Chilterns is under dense tree cover, more than half classified as ancient deciduous woodland.

This age-old protective canopy and lime-rich soil make the Chilterns a haven for bluebells in springtime. Pick any woodland in the Area of Outstanding Natural Beauty that cuts through Berkshire, Buckinghamshire and Hertfordshire and you'll soon stumble upon a flood of brilliant blue.

Highlights include the National Trust's huge Ashridge Estate of woodland and commons above Berkhamsted, Cowleaze Wood, where the bluebells complement a permanent sculpture trail and Wendover Wood, which has beguiling views across the Vale of Aylesbury. Wendover also hosts a Go Ape! highwire forest adventure course for those who need more action than a walk in the woods to enjoy these magical flowers.

Bluebells certainly aren't the only joy of spring to spot while sauntering across the Chilterns. Look up, and you may well spot a red kite, the thrilling bird of prey reintroduced in the 1990s and now thriving above the chalk downlands. The woods are full of birdsong to lift the spirits while muntjac, roe and fallow deer occasionally dart in front of your path, completing this unspoiled haven.

The entirely useless tower
❯ FARINGDON FOLLY, OXFORDSHIRE

How to get there:

Take the A420 towards
Faringdon following the signs
to Folly Hill. After the Sudbury
House Hotel, turn left and park
on the road. The footpath to the
folly is off the high pavement to
the left and is signposted. The
folly is open on the first Sunday
of the month (Easter–Oct).
For sat nav users: SN7 7AQ
Nearest railway station:
Swindon (10 miles)
Bus services:
www.travelinesoutheast.org.uk
0870 6082 608

Find out more:

www.faringdonfolly.org.uk
01634 827 648

Visiting Lord Berners (1883–1950) at his home in Faringdon must have been an odd affair. On the approach to the door of Faringdon House – complete with its sign 'Mangling done here' – your gaze would be distracted by the doves flying from tree to tree. Nothing unusual about that, other than the fact that Lord Berners had coloured them using vegetable dye.

Once inside you would spy pet whippets wearing diamond collars or maybe meet a bowler hat that tottered around the floor under its own power (Berners had trained a parrot to wander around under the hat seemingly to bring it to life). Just when you thought things had settled down for afternoon tea, in would trot Moti, Berners' horse, to join you for a cuppa. Suffice to say that Lord Berners, born Gerald Hugh Tyrwhitt-Wilson, was a great British eccentric. This was a man who claimed to have inherited his title when three of his uncles simultaneously tumbled from a bridge after attending a family funeral (in reality, it was passed on from his grandmother Lady Berners), who would drive around his estate wearing a pig mask to put the wind up the locals, and who daubed moustaches on his family's portraits.

It is only fitting, therefore, that such an idiosyncratic individual would construct England's last traditional folly. In the 18th century, every fashionable landowner worth his salt would construct these completely useless buildings in their grounds. Often based on classical architecture, follies can be found all around Britain: sham temples and castles, obelisks, towers and even, in Dunmore Park, Scotland, a giant stone pineapple.

By the 20th century, the intricacies of planning legislation meant that follies fell from favour but not before Lord Berners constructed his 43-metre brick tower. With dreams of a Gothic masterpiece he went on holiday leaving the project to his architect friend, Lord Gerald Wellesley, insisting that the tower should be 'entirely useless.' The useless tower duly opened in the middle of a fireworks display on 5 November 1935 (with the added spectacle of some red-, white- and blue-dyed doves being released). You can still climb the tower today.

Julia Bradbury on Uffington's White Horse ❯❯

The mist was heavy and atmospheric when we filmed on Lambourn Downs, the series of chalk ridges that straddles the Oxfordshire–Berkshire border, with Uffington to the north and Lambourn in the south. While I was there I had to pay a visit to the famous White Horse at Uffington. The 114-metre long figure, carved into the hillside above the eponymous Vale of the White Horse, is thought to date back 3,000 years.

Considering a quarter of a million visitors tramp up the hillside to see it every year, it looks in remarkably good nick. That's all down to the National Trust wardens who regularly freshen up the chalk. I gave a hand, lugging chalk from a nearby small quarry and crushing it in with a hammer.

There's an old fertility legend that if you walk around the eye three times you fall pregnant. I had to have a go but it didn't work. I think I might have to resort to more traditional methods.

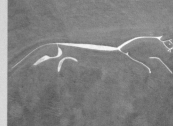

Other things to see:
The Uffington White Horse, 1½ miles south of the village of Uffington, at 114 metres long and 33 metres high, is the largest of Britain's chalk carved horses. It is also the oldest, probably dating from the Bronze Age. As with the Cerne Abbas Giant (see pages 21–23) the National Trust regularly maintains the 1.5–3-metre wide trenches, filling them with up to a metre of chalk to keep the outlines of the horse looking its best.

Lord Berners' eccentric creation, Faringdon Folly (left); the 3,000 year-old Uffington White Horse (above).

Built to defend
❯ BUCKLER'S HARD, HAMPSHIRE

Buckler's Hard, now a pretty harbour but once a major naval shipyard, played a key role in the Battle of Trafalgar and the Second World War.

The picturesque 12-mile long Beaulieu river, running from Lyndhurst to the Solent, has long been a busy thoroughfare. As early as the 13th century, wharves were built at Buckler's Hard to serve the thriving Cistercian monastery founded by King John in 1204, shipping timber from the estate and providing a means for trade with merchants from the continent.

In 1722 ambitious plans were laid to create a new port at Buckler's Hard to import sugar from the West Indies. The new settlement, which was to be named Montagu Town after the 2nd Duke of Montagu, would have consisted of two main boulevards lined with attractive brick houses, a bath-house for the body, a chapel for the soul and an inn for your spirits. Sadly for the Duke, work on the new community foundered when the French got to the Caribbean plantations first, capturing the islands and securing the supply of sugar.

Buckler's Hard would have its revenge on the French sixty years later. From 1745, over 50 of the Royal Navy's finest vessels were constructed here using oak from the New Forest. 5,000 trees were felled to build one man-of-war under the watchful eye of master shipbuilder Henry Adams. The shipyard's finest hour came as the HMS *Euryalus*, HMS *Swiftsure* and the 64-gun HMS *Agamemnon* – Nelson's favourite – sailed into the Battle of Trafalgar.

Sadly, the coming of iron brought with it the demise of wooden shipbuilding at Buckler's Hard. At low tide you can still see the remains of the construction docks poking up from the river bed. As the 19th century gave way to the 20th, Buckler's Hard said farewell to industry and hello to yachtsmen messing around on the water, but with the advent of the Second World War the hamlet was once again called on to help defend the country. Dummy landing craft were built alongside the river ready to be taken to Calais and positioned to make the Nazis believe that a British invasion was about to begin. Later in the war effort, a workforce of 100 men set about constructing segments of the artificial Mulberry Harbour in the old oyster beds at Buckler's Hard. These were towed across the Channel for use in the D-Day landings, while hundreds of boats gathered on the river before making the voyage across to Normandy. You can find out more at the maritime museum.

Today Buckler's Hard has been transformed into a heritage centre, where you can see how life would have been for Henry Adams and his men. It's also one of the few places in the British Isles where you don't pay dues to the Crown to drop anchor. After Henry VIII's dissolution of the monasteries the land and the entire river, including its bed, were passed into the hands of the Montagu family – much to the disgust of the monarchy, which has tried, and failed, to seize control of the river on numerous occasions over the last 500 years.

How to get there:
Exit the M27 at Junction 2 and follow signs for Lyndhurst and then look for brown tourist signs to Beaulieu Village and Buckler's Hard.
For sat nav users: SO42 7XB
Nearest railway station: Beaulieu Road (5½ miles)
No bus services are available but cycle routes run alongside the Beaulieu river from Beaulieu Village.

Find out more:
www.bucklershard.co.uk
01590 616 203

Other things to see:
If you haven't got your sea legs, why not visit Beaulieu Palace House and Abbey, which is also home to the National Motor Museum.
For sat nav users: SO42 7ZN
www.beaulieu.co.uk
01590 612 345

Julia Bradbury goes wild swimming in Oxford »

There are two things I try to avoid: being cold and wet. So, my first reaction to being sent wild swimming in the Thames was: no way. However, on the day of the shoot, the weather was baking and I couldn't resist a dip. I took the plunge in Port Meadow on the outskirts of Oxford where the Thames runs shallow.

It has to be said that swimming in a river is about as different to a swimming-pool experience as you can get. I've never felt so close to nature.

Of course you have to be careful. Even the shallowest water can suddenly deepen and fast currents can soon whisk you off your feet. One of the biggest dangers of wild swimming is slipping on rocks so I was advised either to go barefoot or wear rubber-soled plimsolls to get a better grip. I must admit, putting my bare feet on the river bed wasn't something I particularly enjoyed: you never know what you're standing on. I know I was unlikely to stumble upon a deadly python in Oxford but it still gave me a shiver. Better to be safe than sorry, I guess.

Britain's biggest Christmas tree

❯ WAKEHURST PLACE, WEST SUSSEX

Ever hung your Christmas tree lights only to be disappointed when one bulb blows knocking out the entire thing? Luckily the decorators of the UK's largest living Christmas tree don't have the same problem.

Festive decorations on an industrial scale can be found at Wakehurst Place, home of Kew Gardens' Millennium Seed Bank. Of course, this isn't your common-or-garden Christmas tree but a 35-metre California Redwood. It takes five tree experts two whole days to hang the 1,800 energy-saving bulbs around 12 spirals that are suspended around the tree on a frame much like a Victorian skirt to minimise damage to the trunk or branches. When illuminated, the seasonal display can be seen for miles around and is even visible to pilots coming in to land at Gatwick Airport.

The appeal of Wakehurst lasts long after the decorations have been put back in their boxes. Leased from the National Trust by the Royal Botanic Gardens, Kew, in 1965, 16th-century Wakehurst Place is surrounded by 188 hectares (465 acres) of ornamental and landscaped gardens and conservation areas including four National Collections and rare plants from the southern hemisphere and the Himalayas.

Since the 1970s Wakehurst has also been home to more than a billion seeds in the Millennium Seed Bank. This advanced scientific facility is one of the world's most important

The 35-metre high Wakehurst Christmas tree in all its glory.

Matt Baker **on life in the New Forest »**

One of the things that strikes you as you travel all over the UK for *Countryfile* is how our relatively small country supports so many different ways of life. Take the commoners of the New Forest for example. I visited in 2009 when the New Forest Commoners Defence Association was celebrating its 100th anniversary. This organisation was founded at the turn of the 20th century to protect an ancient way of life and it seems to be working. It's certainly hard to imagine the New Forest without the famous ponies and the pigs that are let out into the forest to eat fallen acorns in the autumn pannage season.

conservation projects, a botanical ark that stores the planet's rarest plants in suspended animation. Seeds arrive from all around the globe and are dried, cleaned and stored in underground freezers at temperatures of –20°C. Currently, samples of 10 per cent of the planet's species are safely banked and the aim is to have a quarter of all plants within Wakehurst's vaults by 2020. With roughly 300,000 known species of plant on Earth this is a herculean task, but one that the Royal Botanic Gardens, Kew, believe is necessary. If climate change continues at its predicted rate, it is likely that 30 per cent of all plant species could become extinct over the course of this century. The seeds frozen deep beneath Wakehurst Place may be our only hope of repopulating the forests, fields and farms of the 22nd century.

Other things to see:

The Millennium Seed Bank parterres represent four threatened habitats near Wakehurst Place itself and four that occur elsewhere in the UK, including marsh and fenland, hills and mountains. In contrast to the high-tech Seed Bank, the Sir Henry Price and Pleasaunce walled gardens are an oasis of calming nostalgia.

How to get there:

From M23, exit at Junction 10 and take the A264 towards East Grinstead and follow the brown tourist signs. Wakehurst Place is open from 10am every day, except 24 and 25 Dec. For sat nav users: RH17 6TN Nearest railway station: Haywards Heath (6 miles) Bus services: www.metrobus.co.uk 01293 449 191

Find out more:

www.kew.org/visit-wakehurst 01444 894 066

Kew Gardens' Millennium Seed Bank and parterres.

A taste of history

> ### ▶ WEALD AND DOWNLAND
> ### OPEN AIR MUSEUM, WEST SUSSEX

How to get there:

Weald and Downland Open Air
Museum is found on the A286.
Open daily Mar–Dec, weekends
and Wed only Jan–Feb.
For sat nav users: PO18 0EU
Nearest railway station:
Chichester (7 miles)
Bus services:
www.stagecoachbus.com
0871 200 22 33

Find out more:

www.wealddown.co.uk
01243 811 363

Some people collect garden gnomes. Some collect teapots.
Some may even go as far as collecting cars. None of these can
top the mania of a Kent-born university lecturer, Roy Armstrong,
who in 1965 started to collect buildings. Distraught that so
many thatched and wooden buildings were being demolished,
Armstrong set about saving examples of vanishing south-east
vernacular architecture. Two years later the *Worthing Gazette*
ran a feature on a proposed village that would be created in
the south of England. 'The strange thing about the community',
the paper reported, 'is that it would be a museum'. In January
1968 the first building arrived in Armstrong's village of the
past: the timbers of Winkhurst farmhouse, saved from the site
of the Bough Beech Reservoir by Sutton and East Surrey Water
Company, soon joined by the dismantled Upper Beeding Toll
House near Steyning. When the museum opened to the public
in 1970 there were seven buildings, although 40 years later
that number has swelled to 45 and rising, all set in 20 hectares
(50 acres) of parkland. Some are grand – such as Bayleaf, an
impressive timber-framed Tudor farmstead, another rescued
from flooding at Bough Beech Reservoir – while others are
humble cattle-sheds and threshing barns. All reek of history
(some, in the case of the musty 19th-century schoolroom from
West Wittering, more than others).

The buildings aren't set in stone, even after they arrive at the
museum. Winkhurst may have been the first to be erected at
Weald and Downland but in 2001, when fresh evidence came to
light that it was actually a kitchen, the museum deconstructed
it for a second time, painstakingly rebuilding the serving area as it would have been and
repositioning it in a better location. To complete the culinary experience, Tudor recipes such
as sodde – boiled eggs with a mustard sauce – are reinterpreted for the modern palate, using
herbs and vegetables such as kale, turnips and leeks from the museum's gardens.

It isn't just the museum's food and exhibits that can roll back the years. Numerous courses
are offered throughout the season, to help keep traditional skills alive, so there's the chance to
try your hand at dowsing, corn-dolly making, animal tracking or coracle carving.

The medieval village at Weald and Downland Open Air Museum.

Matt Baker on the chalky cliffs of the South Downs »

A while ago I took the lead role of Caractacus Potts in the *Chitty Chitty Bang Bang* musical. There's a moment in the show where Ian Fleming's fabulous flying car soars over Beachy Head. I would sing and dance about the amazing white cliffs in every performance but had never actually seen them.

Countryfile gave me the chance to put that right. Not long after the South Downs were designated Britain's newest National Park, I found myself exploring the famous cliffs that stretch along from Seaford Head to, yes, Beachy Head. It's amazing to think these national icons are eroding at a rate of half a metre a year.

Weirdly, in these days of health and safety you'd think there would be some kind of barrier on the edge, but obviously you can't fence off the bottom of Britain. So you're able just to wander up and look over the edge of our island. It's a humbling feeling.

A perfect Tudor village

> **CHIDDINGSTONE, KENT**

The mysterious Chiding Stone just outside the village of Chiddingstone.

How to get there:

Chiddingstone is off the B2027, accessible from the M23 or M20.
For sat nav users: TN8 7AD
Nearest railway station:
Hildenborough (7 miles)
Bus services:
www.traveline.org.uk
0871 200 22 33

Find out more:

www.chiddingstonecastle.org.uk
01892 870 347

A large, peculiarly shaped sandstone bolder known as the Chiding Stone sits inscrutably in the Eden Valley. The reasons for its unusual name are lost. There have been fanciful explanations that it was an altar where druids sacrificed those who chose to ignore their egregious decrees. Others have suggested that it was the place to which you could drag an overbearing wife for a public dressing-down. The more likely, if humdrum explanation, is that it belonged to a Saxon family by the name of the Chiddings. Whatever its origins, it gave its name to the remarkable little village of Chiddingstone. Walk beneath the half-timbered gables of the Tudor houses that make up this single-street village and you could be forgiven for thinking that the community had missed the last few hundred years. Most buildings were built more than 200 years ago, the post office even dating as far back as 1453. In the 20th century only two additions were made – the village hall and rectory – and the village itself can trace its ancestry to AD 814 when it came into the possession of one of the earliest Archbishops of Canterbury. Over the millennia it has passed through the hands of Thomas Boleyn, father of Anne, the Streatfeild family and, since 1939, the National Trust.

Many of Chiddingtone's houses were levelled to make room for the Tudor manor house that in 1805 was remodelled as a castle by Henry Streatfeild. Today the castle is the only part of Chiddingstone not owned by the National Trust (instead it is managed by an independent charity). Apart from revelling in its own mock-Gothic splendour, the castle houses collections of Buddhist, Egyptian and Japanese antiquities, including exhibits of Edo warrior armour. These oddities are open Sun–Wed from Easter weekend to the last Sunday in September.

Julia Bradbury on Kentish cobnuts »

Do you know what a cobnut is? Neither did half the people I asked in Kent, the cobnut capital of the country. It's one of our most traditional nuts, a cultivated hazelnut that's been eaten here for over 400 years. They're good for you, too. Six cobnuts will give you the same amount of protein as a slab of steak and they're packed with fibre. Unfortunately they've fallen out of fashion in recent years. A century ago over 2,800 hectares (7,000 acres) of Kent were devoted to growing cobnuts; now there's only around 100 hectares (250 acres). When you're visiting Kent, you've got to try one. They're a bit like coconut with a taste somewhere between an apple and a chestnut. Oh, they can be baked into mouthwatering biscuits too.

Other things to see:
The Tudor connection
continues three miles away at
Hever Castle, childhood home
of Anne Boleyn. As befits a
former residence of Henry
VIII's doomed wife, the castle
includes a grisly collection
of instruments of torture
and execution.
For sat nav users: TN8 7NG
www.hevercastle.co.uk

Hever Castle, the
childhood home of
Henry VIII's unfortunate
second wife.

Beautiful island of death
❯ THE ISLE OF THANET, KENT

Think of beautiful British beaches and images of Cornwall will probably be conjured up
in your mind's eye. However, on the other side of the country, the beaches of Thanet certainly
give their Cornish cousins a run for their money. At the time of the Roman occupation, the
Isle of Thanet was separated from the rest of England by the Wantsum Channel, a two-mile
wide stretch of sea. The first bridge was constructed in 1485 and even as recently as the
1700s a ferry gave passage from Sandwich. Originally called Tanatus, a name derived from
the Celtic words *teine* meaning 'fire' and *arth* meaning 'height', beacons would have more
than likely been arranged along the coastline. To the Greeks, Britain and Thanet had a more
baleful reputation. This was 'Ynys Thanatos', the legendary Island of the Dead, from where
it was believed souls were rowed across in unmanned boats. If that sounds like pure myth,
Thanet is an archaeological hotspot, with more Bronze Age burial mounds than anywhere
else in Britain.

How to get there:
The Isle of Thanet can
be reached via the M2
or M20, following the
A299 or A258 around
the coast.
For sat nav users: CT9 1EY
Nearest railway stations:
Margate or Ramsgate
Bus services:
www.stagecoachbus.com
0870 243 3711

Other things to see:

Joss Bay is a 200-metre long cove that is popular with surfers. It is said to be named after the 19th-century freetrader Joss Snelling who was so notorious that he was once presented to the future Queen Victoria as 'the famous Broadstairs smuggler'.

Learning to surf in
Joss Bay (above); the
unspoilt, golden sands
of Joss Bay (right).

Dramatic white cliffs, clear water and clean sands at Botany Bay.

As the centuries passed the Wantsum filled with silt and shingle from the River Stour until the isle of the dead finally joined the mainland although it is still referred to as an island. The modern coastline is dominated by Margate, Broadstairs and Ramsgate, their outskirts blurring together as you drive around the seaboard, but the hidden gems are the smaller beaches spotted between, seven of which have been awarded international Blue Flag standard for their clean water and litter-free environments. Only Cornwall beats this tally with eight.

The reason that gorgeously secluded beaches such as Walpole, Minnis and Botany Bay clean up with awards such as these is in part thanks to the volunteer coastal wardens that patrol the Thanet coast. Launched in 2004, the scheme sees each warden adopting a stretch of the coastline, monitoring it for both human and bird activity. This information is then fed back to the Kent Wildlife Trust and put into use for such activities as Seashore Safari rock-pooling events. The result is more responsibility and ownership of the coast, and ultimately cleaner, more environmentally friendly beaches. The area is also a Site of Special Scientific Interest and a National Nature Reserve, and is vitally important to over-wintering birds such as turnstones. These waders return to Thanet from Arctic Canada every winter and rely on being able to roost undisturbed so that they can build up the energy reserves needed for their remarkable journey back home.

Find out more:

www.visitthanet.co.uk

0870 264 6111

Paddle power

❯ CHATHAM, KENT

While paddle steamers conjure up images of Huckleberry Finn and the Mississippi, these evocative vessels have sailed British waters since 1812 when the *Comet* plied between Glasgow and Greenock. Today, only two paddle steamers still operate in the UK. The *Waverley*, the last ocean-going paddle steamer in the world, regularly navigates the seas around England, Scotland and Wales, while the *Kingswear Castle*, Britain's only remaining coal-fired river paddle steamer, sails from Chatham, Rochester and Strood on the River Medway in Kent.

Originally the *Kingswear Castle* was built for very different waters. Commissioned to replace another steamer of the same name, she joined the fleet on the River Dart in Devon in 1924, powered by the steam engine from the original *Kingswear Castle*.

Her voyages along the Dart continued until the 1960s, interrupted only by the Second World War, when she was chartered by the American navy to ferry supplies and personnel to and from Dartmouth.

By the mid-1960s, the popularity of the British seaside holiday was waning. In her heyday, the *Kingswear Castle* carried 400 passengers at a time, but with demand dwindling she found herself joining hundreds of redundant steamers up and down the country. Her bunkers, which once carried up to four tonnes of coal to produce the head of steam, were cleared and 41 years after her maiden voyage, the *Kingswear Castle* made what could have been her last, to Old Mill Creek at Dartmouth. There she would have stayed, slowly rotting away, were it not for the Paddle Steamer Preservation Society purchasing her in 1965 for £600 and raising money for her restoration. In 1985 she was relaunched, this time along the Medway. Modern health-and-safety concerns mean the number of passengers carried has been reduced to 235, but when you stand on deck you cannot help but be transported to an age when the journey itself meant far more than the speed it took to get to your destination.

Britain's oldest working coal-fired river paddle steamer, the *Kingswear Castle* is a fun, leisurely way to take in the Medway and its riverside castles.

How to get there:
The *Kingswear Castle* paddle steamer is berthed in the Historic Dockyard, Chatham, and is signposted from the M2. For sat nav users: ME4 4SX Nearest railway station: Gillingham (1 mile) Bus services: www.arriva.co.uk 0871 200 22 33

Find out more:
www.heritagesteamers.co.uk 01634 827 648

Other things to see:
The Medway is dominated by one of the tallest keeps in Great Britain, guarding an important crossing point. Rochester Castle and its 34-metre high keep dates from the 11th century and has suffered three sieges in its history. Thankfully, plans to demolish the castle in the 18th century came to nothing and so one of the finest examples of Norman fortresses still exists today. For sat nav users: ME1 1QQ www.english-heritage.org.uk 01634 402 276

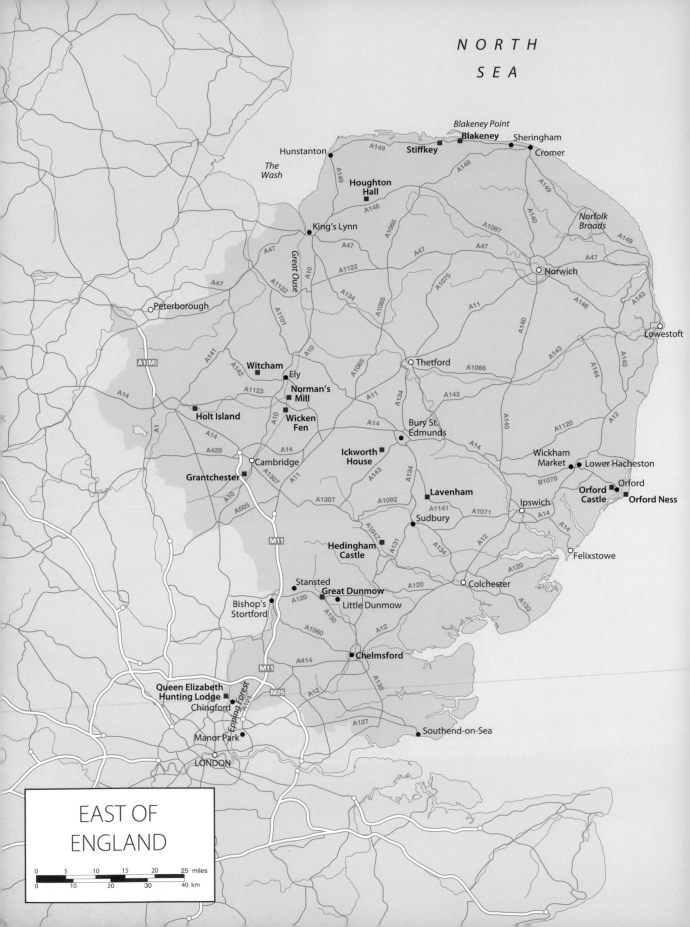

NORTH SEA

Blakeney Point
Blakeney Sheringham
Stiffkey Cromer
A149
Hunstanton
A148
The Wash
A149 **Houghton Hall**
A148
A1065
A1067
Norfolk Broads
King's Lynn
A47 A47 A149
A10 A1122
Great Ouse A47 A47 A47
A1123 A134 Norwich A47
A1122 A1065
A1101 A1075
A141 A1065 A11 A140 A146 A143
A47 A142 **Witcham** A143 Lowestoft
A1(M) Ely A1065 Thetford A1066
A1123 **Norman's** A11 A143 A145
A10 **Mill** A11 A134 A144
Holt Island A14 **Wicken** A14 A140 A12
A1 A10 **Fen** A14 A140
A428 A14 Bury St. A1120
Edmunds
A14 **Ickworth** A143 A134 **Wickham**
Cambridge **House** **Market** Lower Hacheston
A1307 A143 A134 B1078
Grantchester A11 A1092 **Lavenham** Orford
A10 A1307 A1141 **Orford** Orford
A505 A1071 Ipswich **Castle** **Ness**
M11 A1017 Sudbury
A131 A14
Hedingham A131 A134 A12 A14
Castle A134 Felixstowe
Stansted A120 A120
Great Dunmow Colchester
A120 Little Dunmow A12
Bishop's A130
Stortford A12 A133
A1060
A414 A12
Chelmsford
M11 A130
M25
Queen Elizabeth
Hunting Lodge A121
Chingford *Epping Forest* A127 Southend-on-Sea
Manor Park
LONDON
Peterborough

East

Sail through the Broads watching families enjoying the water left, right and centre, and it's hard to imagine a time when the great washes of the East were wild and lawless lands. Only the hardiest lived here, considered by the ruling classes to be little more than animals, amphibious creatures living a harsh lifestyle; where no gentleman feared to tread.

Over time man decided that enough was enough, draining away the water to create fertile farmland. Today, conservationists are trying to reverse the trend, re-establishing fenland in places such as Wicken, letting the water reclaim the land.

Elsewhere in the East, we have continued to try to control landscape, be that the royal hunting grounds of Epping Forest or nuclear test sites in the bleak spits of Orford Ness. Again wildlife has won out, as the once bustling port of Blakeney bears witness. When the estuary began to silt up, the ocean-going vessels of the past could no longer make harbour and the townfolk were forced to adapt to survive.

The battle between sea and land will no doubt continue for generations to come.

The love judge

❯ GREAT DUNMOW, ESSEX

How to get there:

Leave the M11 at Junction 8a
and take the A120 following
signs for Great Dunmow.
For sat nav users: CM6 2AE
Nearest railway stations:
Stansted (5 miles),
Bishop's Stortford (11 miles)
Bus services:
www.firstgroup.com
0871 200 22 33

Find out more:

www.visitessex.com
01932 868 113

Great Dunmow is a town that not only prides itself on happy marriages, but is also determined to prove that it is home to true love. Every four years people flock from miles around to take part in a strange and ancient tradition where couples who have been married for a year and a day are tried by judge and jury to prove that they have never wished themselves single again. And the prize for marital harmony? A flitch of bacon, which is half a salted pig.

No one really knows where or how the tradition started although legend states that the custom originated in the village of Little Dunmow some three miles away. In 1104, a year after their marriage, the lord and lady of the manor disguised themselves as commoners and visited the prior to receive a blessing on their union. The monk was so moved by the strange couple's devotion to each other that he rewarded them with a flitch of bacon. Touched by the gift, the lord revealed his true identity and donated his riches to the priory on one condition: a flitch of bacon would be given to any other couple who could prove that their love was true.

News of the tradition spread throughout the land – even Chaucer mentioned the trials in his *Wife of Bath's Prologue and Tale* – although it wasn't until 1445 that winners were first recorded. Claimants apply to participate six months before the trials, which today take place every leap year, and the five couples to face the jury are selected by the vicar, mayor and judge of Great Dunmow. On the day of the courts, each trial begins with the couple in question kneeling before the jury of six local maidens and six bachelors, the judge and two counsels. They are then grilled over the nature of their marriage and if they are found to share true love they take home the bacon and are carried through the town to take a solemn oath.

And what if they are found guilty of less than wedded bliss? Then they leave to lick their wounds and take the consolation prize – a lump of gammon.

High tide over the
saltmarshes at Blakeney
on the north Norfolk
coast (previous page);
the couple who have
proved their love at the
Great Dunmow love
trials are carried through
the town (right).

Other things to see:
Visit one of the finest Norman keeps in all of England. Hedingham Castle near Braintree stages a number of events every year, including an annual jousting tournament. For sat nav users: CO9 3DJ www.hedinghamcastle.co.uk 01787 460 261

The prize for true love:
half a salted pig.

Hunters and highwaymen

❯ EPPING FOREST, ESSEX

How to get there:

The best place to start exploring Epping Forest is from the Visitor Centre. Exit the M25 at Junction 26, take the A121 and follow the signs.

For sat nav users: IG10 4AE

Nearest railway station: Chingford (3½ miles)

Bus services:

www.tfl.gov.uk

0843 222 1234

The forest can also be accessed from several London Underground stations (see www.tfl.gov.uk for details)

Find out more:

www.cityoflondon.gov.uk/epping

020 8508 0028

For a bustling metropolis, London is blessed with many green spaces but none is as striking as Epping Forest, stretching from Manor Park in East London to Epping in Essex. Nearly 2,400 hectares (6,000 acres) are covered by the forest which is, in fact, a rich mosaic of habitats including heath, rivers, grasslands and over 80 lakes and ponds.

Epping Forest first appears in official records in 1662, although its history can be traced back long before the Roman occupation. The Saxons are said to have been the first to settle beneath its trees and over the years it has been known as Ippying, Eppinghethe and Eppingthorpe.

In the 12th century, Henry III made the forest a royal hunting ground, a designation that allowed commoners to gather food and fuel within its boundaries but only the crown could hunt its boar and deer. Both Henry VIII and his daughter Elizabeth I chased quarry through its glades and in the 18th century the Forest became the haunt of the infamous highwayman Dick Turpin. Far from being the dashing romanticised figure of popular culture, Turpin was a short, smallpox-scarred robber who lived rough in a cave, ready to pounce on any victim and regularly torturing local women.

In 1870, the tolls on the roads through Epping Forest were lifted, but the City of London was concerned that open countryside around the capital was increasingly threatened by London's expansion. In order to protect the forest, the Epping Forest Act 1878 placed the woodland in the hands of the Corporation of London. Four years later Queen Victoria dedicated the forest 'to the enjoyment of my people forever'.

And enjoy it we do. With over 50,000 trees, including ancient oak, beech and hornbeam, the Forest provides a delightful backdrop and breathing space. And the reason we can enjoy so many trees is down to the practice carried out by thousands of commoners over the centuries of pollarding the trees, cutting them back at a height that is out of reach of grazing animals. The technique, still widely used by conservationists, extends the life of a tree and promotes growth, meaning that Epping Forest may be around for many more centuries.

The 16th-century Queen Elizabeth Hunting Lodge, first enjoyed by guests of Henry VIII (right); Beech trees in autumn, Epping Forest (opposite).

Other things to see:

The Queen Elizabeth Hunting Lodge was built by Henry VIII in 1543 so that visiting nobles could stand at its windows taking pot-shots at passing deer. Entrance to the Lodge is free and includes displays on Tudor food and kitchenware. The Lodge is a five-minute walk from Chingford station.

For sat nav users: E4 7QH

020 8529 6681

Take your best shot
❯ WITCHAM, CAMBRIDGESHIRE

How to get there:

The village of Witcham is found off the A142. The World Peashooting Championship takes place every July on the second Saturday and 2010 will be the 40th holding of the event. If you fancy your chances, turn up at 1pm for the 2pm shoot-out.

For sat nav users: CB6

Nearest railway station: Ely (5 miles)

Bus services: www.traveline.org.uk 0871 200 22 33

Find out more:

www.witcham.org.uk 01932 868 113

In 1971, as the villagers of Witcham were scratching their heads for ways to raise funds for their newly constructed village hall, John Tyson, the local headmaster, caught a number of his pupils testing their new pea-shooters. A novel thought struck him. Could the plague of his playground put cash into the community coffers? A competition to find the surest pea-shot was staged at the next village fair and became an instant hit.

The task is simple. Contestants have five chances to strike a target 4 metres away. One point is awarded for a pea in the outer ring, three for the middle and five for the bull's-eye. Those players in the top sixteen places on the leader board then shoot it out among them until the two grand finalists go head to head in the mother of all lung-powered duels.

The contest is taken extremely seriously by the contestants, some of whom travel from as far as New Zealand. As the day goes on you can hear mutterings about the right level of wind expenditure (how hard you blow, in layman's terms) or the critical moisture criteria (the ideal amount of saliva to leave on the poor pea). True pros use dried maple seeds instead of peas, while traditionalists ensure that their legume is no more than 5.5mm in diameter, so as to avoid an embarrassing – and time-wasting – blockage in their pipe.

Recent years have also brought controversy when laser-guided pea-shooters fitted with gyroscopic balancing devices were introduced by experts from the nearby RAF Lakenheath US air force base. Arguments have broken out over whether these new high-tech weapons should be allowed, but in the spirit of Mr Tyson, an uneasy peas-treaty has been called.

World Champion pea-shot George Hollis and his adapted peashooter with gyroscopic balancing system and hyper-accurate laser sight.

Other things to see:
Holt Island, located on the Great Ouse between Hemingford Meadow and The Waits, was once a commercial osier bed, growing willow withies for basket weaving. With a decline in demand for osiers, the 2.8-hectare (7-acre) site is now a nature reserve and home to a variety of wildlife from deer to kingfishers and reed warblers. It is open weekends and bank holidays, Apr–Sept. www.huntsdc.gov.uk

A common kingfisher or
Alcedo atthis.

The last waterland

❯ WICKEN FEN, CAMBRIDGESHIRE

Wicken Fen in summer,
showing the windpump
'Norman's Mill'.

Before the 17th century the Great Fen Basin of East Anglia was a strange and grim place.
The entire area from the Norfolk Wash to Cambridgeshire was a waterlogged wilderness,
formed 5,000 years ago when sea levels rose and the land flooded. When the Romans arrived
they immediately tried to drain the basin, but it remained marshy wetland until the last few
hundred years. A few early settlements, such as Wisbech and Ely, were established by monks
on the rare islands and silt banks, but most of those who eked out a living on the fens were

a sturdy and often wild bunch. Calling themselves the Breedlings, they lived on fish and waterfowl and were often above the law – or rather beyond it, because the law would not venture into the trackless, dangerous fenland. Thus the fens gained a brutal reputation as the ultimate watery hideout for outlaws.

All that changed around 1620 when the Earl of Bedford asked the Dutch reclaimer Sir Cornelius Vermuyden to drain the fens around Ely. Under his guidance, a band of wealthy Dutch entrepreneurs known as the Adventurers set about constructing a system of canals and ditches to transform the wetlands into arable farmland. The Breedlings responded with violence, sabotaging the drainage equipment at every opportunity, but it was a battle they would ultimately lose. Only one per cent of the Great Fen Basin remains, the once inhospitable marshes now transformed into a bountiful breadbasket. One of the four fragments of wild fenland is now Britain's oldest nature reserve, Wicken Fen. As the land was being drained Wicken was recognised by Victorian naturalists as an important remnant of a disappearing ecosystem and at the end of the 19th century the newly formed National Trust was encouraged to buy up land to protect this habitat. In 1899 the Trust snapped up two acres for £10 and over the intervening years their holding has been extended with some farmland being returned to its natural state. Today Wicken Fen covers 360 hectares (900 acres), supporting 8,230 species of bird, plant and insect. The rich peat bog is a haven for invertebrates in particular. Twenty different types of dragonfly strafe across the reeds, including the four-spotted chaser, emperor and various damselflies, while over 1,000 different species of beetle make Wicken Fen their home. No wonder Charles Darwin used to travel to Wicken in the 1820s from his Cambridge chambers to collect the extremely rare crucifix ground beetle, which was recently rediscovered in the reserve. There is larger wildlife to spot as well, most notably the introduced silvery Konik pony, a small, hardy breed, well adapted to wetland habitats, that may be a descendant of the wild horses that once roamed Europe's forests, and a suitably primitive grazer for such an untamed landscape.

Other things to see:

Near the Visitor Centre you'll find the only working example of a wooden windpump on the Fens. Originally known as Norman's Mill, it used to help control the water levels around the peat pits, but it is now used to pump water on to sedge fen, another important habitat, to keep it from drying out.

How to get there:
Wicken Fen is south of the A1123 and can be reached from Cambridge by the A10. For sat nav users: CB7 5XP
Nearest railway station:
Ely (9 miles)
Bus services:
www.stagecoachbus.com
01223 423 578

Find out more:
www.wicken.org.uk
01353 720 274

The windpump at the entrance to Wicken Fen, and the last surviving working wind-pump in the Cambridgeshire fens. It was constructed here in 1956.

Waxing lyrical
▶ GRANTCHESTER, CAMBRIDGESHIRE

'Ah, Grantchester! There's peace and holy quiet there', wrote Rupert Brooke in 1912 in his famous poem 'The Old Vicarage, Grantchester'. Nearly one hundred years later, things haven't changed much. As Cambridge continues to swell ever closer, Grantchester is a place of rumination and woolgathering. It was here, walking across the meadows beside the River Cam that the idea of artificial intelligence first popped into the head of mathematician Alan Turing. Further upstream is Byron's Pool where the romantic Lord is believed to have enjoyed a dip or two, not far away from the spot where American poet Sylvia Plath once performed Chaucer to a rapt audience of nearby cows. The charms of Grantchester were not lost on one of its famous sons: David Gilmour was born here and the place was immortalised in 1969 in the Pink Floyd song 'Grantchester Meadows'.

In 1909 Brooke moved into the village, lodging first at Orchard House and then the Old Vicarage, which gave its name to the poem he wrote while homesick in Germany. Charismatic and bohemian, Brooke gathered around him a close circle of friends – the so-called Grantchester Group – including Virginia Woolf, E. M. Forster and Ludwig Wittgenstein. Here they would picnic, punt and even take skinny-dips in the Cam by moonlight.

Brooke's nostalgic Grantchester poem ends with the words 'Stands the Church clock at ten to three? And is there honey still for tea?' While no one has ever been sure that the clock of St Andrew and St Mary's has ever been stuck at fifty minutes past two, the honey still flows at the famous Orchard Tea Garden. But be warned, the queues are near legendary, and for good reason: Cambridge University's finest have long popped out here for a cuppa, from A.A. Milne and Emma Thompson to Stephen Hawking and John Cleese.

Other things to see:
Find out more about Brooke and his connection to Grantchester at the scintillating Rupert Brooke Museum, open all year around and located next to the Orchard Tea Garden. Admission free.
For sat nav users: CB3 9ND
www.rupertbrookemuseum.org.uk
01223 551 118

How to get there:
Leave the M11 at Junction 12 and follow signs for Grantchester. Of course, you can also punt along the Cam or wander along the mile-long river walk known as Grantchester Grind.
For sat nav users: CB3 9ND
Nearest railway station: Cambridge (3 miles)
Bus services:
www.cambridgeshire.gov.uk/transport
0845 045 0675

Find out more:
www.visitcambridgeshire.org
0871 226 8006

Blossom time in the Orchard Tea Garden, Grantchester.

A common sight

❯ BLAKENEY, NORFOLK

The tranquil village of Blakeney is the perfect place for a potter. Take a meander through streets lined with attractive flint cottages, rest up a while in the ubiquitous country tea-rooms and pubs, or visit the free-to-enter 15th-century Guildhall, with its atmospheric brick-vaulted undercroft. Above the old harbour, the impressive parish church of St Nicholas stands guard over the village with its curious twin towers. But these are not identical twins. The larger of the two points majestically 31 metres into the air, while the second, more spindly, tower on the north east side of the church once housed a beacon to guide those at sea.

This intriguing addition to the church – and the huge galleon in full sail proudly displayed on the village sign – hint at the fact that Blakeney wasn't always quite so sleepy. Up to the 17th century you were as likely to hear Dutch spoken on the streets of Blakeney as English. The now peaceful quay would have been a bustling hive of activity, with boats constantly sailing back and forth from the Flemish community. Step back another 400 years and the village was the fourth most important port in all of England. Corn and wool was exported here, while some of England's finest oysters were landed by Blakeney fishermen. The harbour was a regular point of departure for members of the royal family heading for Flanders and, in the 16th century, the port even dispatched three ships to help fight the Spanish Armada.

How to get there:

Blakeney is found off the A148 Cromer–Hunstanton road.
For sat nav users: NR25 7NW
Nearest railway station: Sheringham (9 miles)
Bus services:
www.travelineeastanglia.org.uk
0871 200 22 33

Find out more:

www.nationaltrust.org.uk/blakeney
01263 740 241

The Blakeney village sign, a clue to the village's nautical past as a major trading port (above); Blakeney harbour (right).

Blakeney's fortunes declined as the estuary began to silt up. Commercial craft could no longer get into harbour and the port found itself marooned with only a meandering creek that wandered for over a mile through salt-flats to the open sea. Today the channel can only be navigated for a few short hours at high tide and the only boats you'll find are pleasure craft, mostly setting out for Blakeney Point, a 3½ mile spit of sand-dunes and shingle.

The Point is one of the largest expanses of undeveloped coastal habitat in Europe and supports a wide array of birdlife, including the little, common and Arctic terns in winter and the Sandwich and common terns in summer. However, most people take a trip to Blakeney Point to see the true stars of the show: common and grey seals. During June and July, the beaches of Blakeney Point are packed with cute, white common seal pups, some as young as four weeks old, brought here by their mothers to be weaned in safety. Sailing folk love this stretch of the Norfolk coast in summer too – in August, Blakeney is host to a colourful regatta, attracting over 50 yachts and their crews.

Other things to see:
Stiffkey, some five miles east of Blakeney, is a pretty base from which to explore the salt-marshes. While you're there, try the local delicacy, its distinctively coloured cockles, known rather appropriately in the region as 'Stewkey Blues'.

Common and grey seals on the sand bar off Blakeney Point.

Prime-ministerial majesty

❯ HOUGHTON HALL, NORFOLK

How to get there:

Houghton Hall is located just off the A148, the King's Lynn to Cromer road. It is open Apr–Sept.

For sat nav users: PE31 6UE

Nearest railway station: King's Lynn (14 miles)

There is no bus service.

Sir Robert Walpole (1676–1745) was a giant in almost every aspect. Corpulent in frame and a colossus in Whitehall – the first man to be regarded as prime minister, effectively running the country for 23 years – Walpole was also a man of monumental aspiration, as can be seen at Houghton Hall, the palatial residence he built near King's Lynn on the Norfolk coast.

Walpole had inherited the relatively modest Houghton Estate in 1700 at the age of 24. Two decades later, the existing Restoration house was demolished and work began on his Palladian mansion. Grand, ornate, some would even say pompous, the house cost well over £200,000, a considerable fortune in his day, plunging the prime minister into debt. Not unduly worried, Walpole began to amass an outstanding collection of over 400 great works of art, which enabled his grandson to put the family back in the black by selling the entire collection to Catherine the Great of Russia in 1779.

The crowning glory of Houghton Hall is the grandiose Stone Hall designed by William Kent. Inspired by Inigo Jones' Queen's House in Greenwich, built for the wife of James I, this all-white double-height hall, galleried on three sides, was the first room you saw on entering Houghton and there is no mistaking the impression it was intended to create. It's no coincidence that Walpole's bust stands considerably higher than the Roman emperors that flank it. The other rooms are similarly luxurious. The Marble Parlour is fittingly dedicated to Bacchus, Greek god of wine, and Walpole's state bed with its giant scallop shell against the head cloth is as grand as the man who would have slept in it. From a surviving bill it is known that the bed and its trimmings cost £1,219 in 1732, the equivalent of £186,000 today.

The Hall is set in 101 hectares (350 acres) of lush parkland, home to a herd of rare white fallow deer. The original two hectare (five acre) walled garden has been divided by tall yew hedges into a number of garden 'rooms', each given a separate identity by different plants and statues. The gardens have recently welcomed a new addition: the Water Flame art installation by Dutch artist Jeppe Hein, in which a fire seems continually to blaze on top of a spout of water. Like all of Houghton, it has to be seen to be believed.

Houghton Hall (opposite); Stone Hall, the elaborate entrance to Houghton Hall (above).

Other things to see:
Houghton Hall also boasts one of the world's largest and most comprehensive collections of model soldiers: over 2,000 wage war against beautifully hand-painted backdrops. The Soldier Museum is found next to the Hall's restaurant.

Find out more:
www.houghtonhall.com
01485 528 569

$\mathcal{M}att$ $\mathcal{B}aker$ celebrates Norfolk's waterways ⟫

As soon as my Grandpa found out we were filming on the Norfolk Broads he began telling me about the times he took my Mum there as a child on holiday. 'You'll love it', he promised.

We were filming on the May bank holiday and the Broads were heaving. One of my personal highlights was heading out on a traditional wherry. These clinker-built vessels, with their huge single sails, were the lorries of yesteryear, transporting goods through the Broads. As the rail networks took over, the wherries were transformed into pleasure cruisers, the last trading wherry, the *Ella*, launching in 1912.

What a fantastic way to explore the Broads today, to be part of the crew hoisting that massive sail. Everywhere we went we saw families enjoying the water. It felt like a real celebration. Grandpa was right. I loved it.

Relic of the cold war

❯ ORFORD NESS, SUFFOLK

A view of the twin pagodas from the saltings, west of Stony Ditch at Orford Ness. The pagodas were built by the AWE (Atomic Weapons Establishment) to house testing sites.

Today the 9½ mile shingle spit of Orford Ness is a wildlife heaven but just 40 years ago some would have described it as hell. Where marsh harriers and barn owls swoop, tests on Britain's first atomic bomb were carried out on this lonely beach and the relics of Orford's top-secret military history litter the stretches of shingle, decaying monuments to the UK's war efforts in the 20th century.

Most striking are the ramshackle concrete pagodas that housed experiments to see how our nuclear weapons would cope with extreme temperatures, vibrations and G-forces.

Standing here, as the wind whistles through the rusting structures, it is sobering to realise that Blue Danube, the UK's first nuclear missile, would have been lowered by a 10-tonne crane into a pit right beneath your feet before being subjected to vibrations to see what would occur. Originally the test-cell was topped by an aluminum roof, designed to blow off in the event of an accident. Later scientists would have been relieved to see reinforced concrete lids replacing the seemingly flimsy metal covering.

The site also housed Anglo-American classified experiments such as Cobra Mist, codename for an 'over-the-horizon' radar system that attempted to keep an eye on the Soviets and Russians. But to this day, conspiracy theorists believe that something more extraordinary was happening in the huddle of dull, grey hangars. Was the official story about Cobra Mist a cover for experimentation on crashed alien spaceships and the monitoring of UFOs across Britain? The truth, as the *X-Files* insisted, is out there, but at present the only technology located at Cobra Mist are the BBC's World Service transmitters.

There's no escaping the fact that the bleak, vegetated shingle does have an extra-terrestrial feel to it, emphasised in part by its shabby cold-war skeletons. There have been tales of the unexplained here for centuries. In 1749, the *Gentleman's Magazine* ran a report that local fishermen had been attacked and killed by a winged, crocodile-like sea-dragon that they had snared in their nets. The wildlife now found on Orford Ness is slightly more conventional although impressive. The cry of curlews is often on the air, while oystercatchers and redshank gather in noisy flocks. The distinctive black and white avocet often makes an appearance, darting between the yellow horned poppy that grows in the sand and shingle of Suffolk's shoreline.

Befitting this other-worldly environment, access to the spit is via a National Trust ferry, but once on the spit, with its seemingly endless paths, you can enjoy the same solitude that made it such an ideal location for a nuclear-testing ground.

How to get there:
Leave the A12 at Lower Hacheston, following the B1078 to Orford Quay in Orford for the ferry (crossings between 10am and 2pm only) to the Ness. For sat nav users: IP12 2NU Nearest railway station: Wickham Market (8 miles) Bus services: www.suffolkonboard.com 0845 606 6171

Find out more:
www.nationaltrust.org.uk/orfordness
01728 648 024

Other things to see:
Orford Castle was built by Henry II in the 1160s to keep the treacherous barons of Norfolk and Suffolk under control, and to ward off coastal invaders. It has a unique 21-sided tower, from the top of which there are impressive views over Orford Ness. The castle is said to the home of one of the UK's weirdest ghosts, the grunting spirit of a merman who allegedly was kept prisoner in the dungeons around 1204.
For sat nav users: IP12 2ND
www.orford.org.uk
01394 450 472

The 12th-century Orford Castle.

Wonky town
❯ LAVENHAM, SUFFOLK

How to get there:

Lavenham is on the A1141, between Sudbury and Bury St Edmunds.

For sat nav users: CO10 9RA

Nearest railway station: Sudbury (7 miles)

Bus services:

www.chamberscoaches.co.uk

01787 227 233

Find out more:

www.lavenham.co.uk

01787 248 207

Lavenham is the town that time forgot, a labyrinth of narrow streets lined with brightly coloured, half-timbered houses leaning drunkenly against each other. But what we see today as romantic and even quaint was the nearest that medieval Britain got to bling. The reason that the town has a grand total of 361 listed buildings is that the merchants of Lavenham wanted to show off. During the reign of Edward III the modestly sized town was a major exporter of woollen cloth, specifically Lavenham Blue, its famous woad-dyed broadcloth, which was even sent as far afield as North Africa and Russia. The merchants of the day were justifiably proud of their success and many even ripped down their homes to rebuild them in the most flamboyant and fashionable styles they could. The town's zenith came in 1524 when it was named as the 14th richest town in the Kingdom, paying more tax than large cities such as York and Lincoln. Such were the riches of Lavenham, the town could even afford to install a covered culvert system in the 1520s – almost unheard of in the 16th century.

The market place is dominated by the lime-washed Guildhall, constructed in 1529, and as higgledy-piggledy as the rest of the town. Built by the Guild of Corpus Christi, one of the three guilds that regulated the cloth trade in Lavenham, it has acted as a prison, workhouse and wool store in its time, even housing evacuees during the Second World War. Now in the hands of the National Trust, it contains a local history museum.

The single-most impressive monument to Lavenham's success, however, is the opulent Church of St Peter and St Paul that dominates the skyline. Completed around 1530 this is a typical example of Suffolk's 'wool churches', places of worship that now appear far too imposing for their modest surroundings.

Of course, all good things must come to an end. In 1525, Henry VIII began to impose heavy taxes on the wool trade to finance his wars with France. This check on Lavenham's fortunes coincided exactly with a period in which cheaper cloth began to be imported from Europe. Within 40 years, Lavenham faced commercial ruin, refusing to move with the times while industrious neighbours progressed. After 1530 there was no mercantile wealth reflected in the quality of the buildings. So, when you walk around this delightful medieval market town, be aware that you're strolling through a 16th-century economic-disaster area.

Other things to see:

Ickworth House, 13 miles from Lavenham, is one of the most unusual stately homes in Britain, befitting the nature of its eccentric creator, Frederick, 4th Earl of Bristol and Bishop of Derry. An outsized rotunda dominates this Italianate Georgian palace, which is surrounded by formal Italian gardens and extensive parkland created partly by Capability Brown.
For sat nav users: IP29 5QE
www.nationaltrust.org.uk/ickworth
01284 735 270

The brightly coloured timber houses of Lavenham (opposite and above); the central rotunda of Ickworth House, designed by Italian architect Mario Asprucci (left).

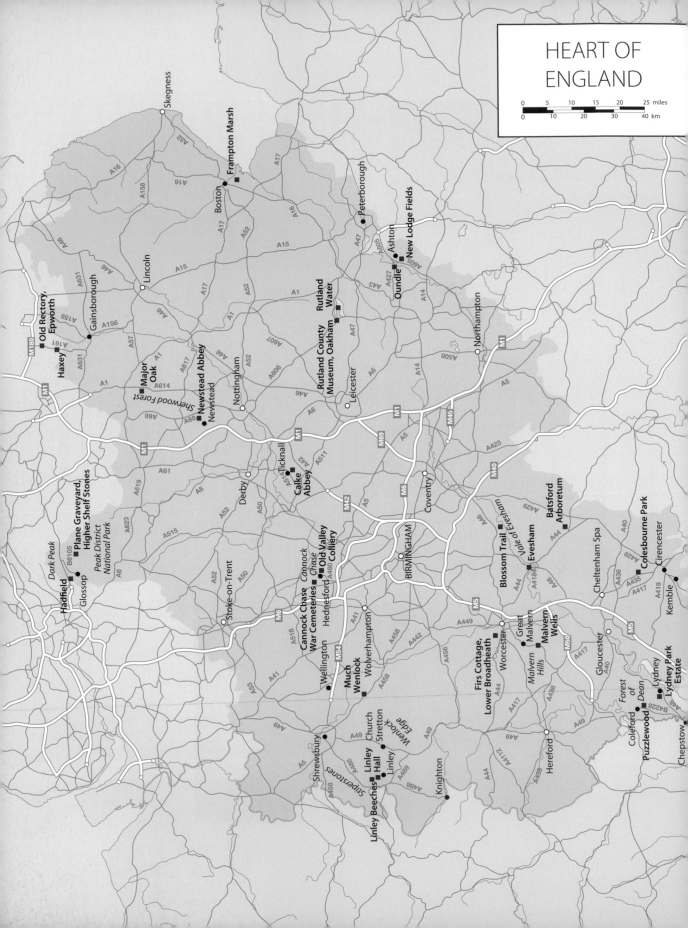

0   5   10   15   20   25 miles
0   10   20   30   40 km

Skegness

Frampton Marsh

A52

A16

A158

A16

A17

A17

Boston

A52

Peterborough

A47

A605

Ashton

New Lodge Fields

A605

A16

A17

A15

A1

A427

Oundle

A14

Lincoln

A15

A46

A631

Gainsborough

A156

A46

A57

A46

A1

A607

Rutland
Water

Rutland County
Museum, Oakham

A47

Northampton

A508

M1

Old Rectory,
Epworth

M180

A161

A159

Haxey

A631

A1

Major
Oak

A617

A614

Newstead Abbey

Sherwood Forest

A60

Newstead

Nottingham

A46

A52

A6

Leicester

A6

A5

A14

M1

A60

A60

A61

M1

A619

A623

Dark Peak

B6105

Plane Graveyard,
Higher Shelf Stones

Glossop

Peak District
National Park

A6

A515

A52

A50

A6

A623

Derby

A50

A511

A42

Ticknall

Calke
Abbey

M1

M69

A46

M45

A423

M40

A5

Batsford
Arboretum

A429

Colesbourne Park

A40

Cirencester

Hadfield

A57

Stoke-on-Trent

A52

A50

A515

Cannock Chase
War Cemeteries

Cannock
Chase

Old Valley
Colliery

A460

Hednesford

M6

A5

Coventry

BIRMINGHAM

M6

M42

A5

Blossom Trail

A4184

Vale of Evesham

Evesham

A44

Cheltenham Spa

A436

A435

A429

A419

Kemble

A518

M6

A41

Wellington

M54

Much
Wenlock

Wolverhampton

A458

A458

A442

A456

A449

M5

Firs Cottage,
Lower Broadheath

A44

Worcester

Great
Malvern

Malvern
Wells

Malvern
Hills

A38

M50

A417

Gloucester

A40

A417

A46

M5

A53

A41

Wellington

Shrewsbury

A5

A49

Church
Stretton

Wenlock
Edge

Linley Beeches

Linley
Hall

Linley

A488

A49

Knighton

A49

A44

Hereford

A4112

A438

A49

Forest
of
Dean

Coleford

Puzzlewood

Lydney

Lydney Park
Estate

B4228

A48

Chepstow

Stiperstones

A488

A488

Heart of England

The Heart of England is that timeless realm so beloved of jigsaw makers. Here the sun always shines, the roses always bloom in the gardens of thatched cottages and horse and carts clatter down narrow lanes. OK, so reality isn't always like that, but the dream of the rural idyll is never too far from you in this great swathe of central England. This was land built on the fortunes of the wool industry, where cider-apple blossom burst into life each spring and the hills gave up crystal-clear water that could cleanse body, mind and spirit. It has given us great eccentrics from Lord Byron to the compulsive hoarders of Calke Abbey and the curious hunters of the Haxey Hood.

Here you can experience successes in both flora and fauna, from the first sign of snowdrops at Colesbourne Park to the magnificent ospreys over Rutland Water or take to the hills of the Peak District, the UK's first National Park. Truly the stuff that dreams are made of.

The plane graveyard
❯ DARK PEAK, DERBYSHIRE

How to get there:

Higher Shelf Stones is a 7 mile walk from Glossop. It's a route that should only be attempted by experienced walkers in good weather conditions. It can be found on the Ordnance Survey Landranger 110 map.

Find out more:

www.visitpeakdistrict.com
01457 869 176

In the north of the Peak District National Park lies Dark Peak, a forbidding but beautiful blanket-bog moorland, dotted with bizarrely shaped boulders with magical names: Back Tor, the Cakes of Bread and Salt Cellar. It's not surprising to discover that such dramatic landscape has inspired dramatic legends and Dark Peak is awash with stories linking the region with the denizens of hell. The Devil's Elbow, a curved section of the B6105, is said to be built on the calcified remains of Satan's arm after Old Nick had his limb turned to stone by God when he was caught trying to drag two lovers down to the underworld. In a fury, Lucifer tore it clean off and left it there. Ever since the area has become known as a place of uncanny occurrences, from mysterious lights in the sky to tales of a giant shadowy slug that is said to slither and slide across the moor.

However, the greatest mystery has nothing to do with demons or gastropods. Between the 1930s and 1950s over 50 planes crashed into these hills in mysterious circumstances. With over 130 airmen losing their lives, the area has understandably become known as the Bermuda Triangle of Britain and you can still see the remains of the fallen craft scattered across the unforgiving peaks.

One of the best-preserved wrecks in this plane graveyard lies near Glossop. On 3 November 1948, 'Overexposed', a B29 Superfortress of the 16th Photographic Reconnaissance Squadron, was en route to RAF Burtonwood in Warrington, the largest airfield in Europe at that time. The aircraft ploughed into the hillside at Higher Shelf Stones and burst into flames, killing all 13 of the crew. All four engines can still be seen alongside the twisted undercarriage and fragments of metal.

But what repeatedly caused planes to crash? Was it the ghosts of the Dark Peak's satanic past or rogue magnetic forces from the rocks themselves? The truth is slightly more prosaic. Most of the planes that met their doom on the moors weren't even supposed to be flying there. Some were diverted due to bad weather, some were just plain lost and others, sadly, seem to have taken to the skies over Dark Peak because their inexperienced pilots were showing off or even giving their friends a lift home. In a place known for low cloud cover and at a time when sophisticated navigation systems had yet to be invented, the only way for them to get their bearings was to drop below the clouds to spot landmarks. Unfortunately, in such rugged terrain they were nearer to the landmarks than they thought.

Other things to see:

In 1999 a new comedy series about a fictional north-country community was produced for the BBC, first on Radio 4 and then as a television series for BBC2 further adding to the weirdness of the Dark Peak region. *The League of Gentlemen* has become a cult favourite and its fans flock to Hadfield, a village 2 miles from Glossop, to seek out the locations frequented by locals of the fictional Royston Vasey.

Win Hill's summit as the sun rises over the Peak District. Kinder Scout Plateau can be seen on the horizon (above); The 'Local Shop' from the set of *The League of Gentlemen*, Marsden Moor, Hadfield (left).

A place of remembrance
❭ CANNOCK CHASE, STAFFORDSHIRE

How to get there:
Leave the M6 at Junction 11
and take the A460, following
signs for Cannock Chase.
For sat nav users: WS12 4PW
Nearest railway station:
Hednesford (2½ miles)
Bus Services:
www.arrivabus.co.uk
0871 200 22 33

Cannock Chase is an Area of Outstanding Natural Beauty that covers 26 square miles of open countryside. Today, its visitors can enjoy wandering over vast areas of heath and woodland but during the two world wars the landscape would have looked very different. The rough terrain had been used as military training grounds since 1870 and between 1914 and 1918 around half a million British and Commonwealth troops passed through two camps, Brocton, near Anson's Bank, and Rugeley, along Penkridge Bank, on the way to the trenches.

After the Great War, the camps were demolished although one hut survived and was transferred 3 miles to Gayton to become the village community hall. When the villagers received lottery funding to build a new centre 85 years later, the hut was once again saved from being torn down and returned to the Chase. Fitted out to how it would have appeared in 1916, the refurbished hut gives a rare insight into the life of servicemen preparing for the front.

By the Second World War, the Chase was the home of RAF Hednesford, which opened in 1939. Here, at any one time, around 2,000 men and women received basic training on the maintenance of aircraft before being posted around the countryside. Nothing remains of the base today. The buildings, which included a cinema, churches and, uniquely, a Jewish synagogue, briefly became a centre for square-bashing National Service trainees in the 1950s but were bulldozed in the 60s to become part of the Cannock Chase Country Park.

Memorials to those who fought on both sides of the world wars can still be found in Cannock Chase. The Commonwealth Military Cemetery is the final resting place for members of the New Zealand Rifle Brigade – based here during the First World War – and German prisoners of war from the local military hospitals. Not far away is the German Military Cemetery. The area was sold to the German War Graves Commission in 1959 for the princely sum of five acorns. It contains the graves of nearly 5,000 Germans, men who were shot down during air raids, washed up on British beaches or drowned in Nazi submarines, all buried together as they died on British soil. The last person to be interred here was Lieutenant Werner Knittel who was shot down over Romney Marshes in October 1940. His body was finally discovered by aviation archaeologists 33 years later and laid to rest alongside his countrymen. Here, in this unique and touching location, wartime enemies lie in peace just a few miles from each other.

Find out more:
www.visitcannockchase.co.uk
01543 464 523

Other things to see:
The Museum of Cannock Chase explores the area's industrial past. Based at the old Valley Colliery where young men trained before heading down to a life underground, the museum also covers the Chase's military past. Admission is free. For sat nav users: WS12 1TD www.cannockchasedc.gov.uk/ museum
01543 877 666

The birth of the Olympic Games

❯ MUCH WENLOCK, SHROPSHIRE

Athens was undoubtedly the birthplace of the ancient Olympics in 776 BC, but the origins of the modern games can be traced to the narrow streets of a Shropshire market town.

Much Wenlock is the quintessential country community, full of picturesque timber-framed Tudor, Jacobean and Georgian buildings and the site of an evocative 12th-century Cluniac abbey. However, most people come here to walk the mile-and-a-half Olympic trail, which tells the story of the Wenlock Olympian games. The sporting event was organised in October 1850 by the town's doctor, William Penny Brookes, who saw it as a great opportunity to improve the physical and mental mettle of his neighbours. The bewhiskered MD also wanted to introduce an alternative to the townfolk's main pastime: a drink down the pub.

The games were a mix of athletics and local traditional sports such as football, cricket and quoits. To amuse and attract people to take part, Brookes also included more left-field pursuits including wheelbarrow and penny-farthing races, a 50-yard hop and even knitting. Pageantry was as important in Wenlock as in today's international games. The opening ceremony included marches, bands and flag-waving and soon folk started to travel from wide and far to take part.

The German Military Cemetery at Cannock Chase (opposite); the exterior of Raynald's Mansion in Much Wenlock. The timber-framed building dates from 1682 (below).

Brookes went on to found Liverpool's National Olympian Association in 1865. Their first festival was a resounding success, attracting crowds of over 10,000 spectators. It was so successful that those who were convinced that athletics should remain the pursuit of private school and university graduates formed a rival society, which paved the way for today's ruling athletics body in Great Britain.

Such was the reputation of this humble country doctor, that a Frenchman, Baron Pierre de Coubertin, visited the Wenlock games in 1890 to meet the man who shared his dream of organising an international Olympic Games. Baron de Coubertin would go on to realise that dream, but unfortunately Brookes did not live to see it: he died just four months before the first Olympic Games were held in Athens in 1896.

While London works towards hosting the 2012 Olympics, the Wenlock games are still held every July. The events, including fencing, archery and golf, may be more conservative than Brookes' original games and the locations, Linden Fields and the local Sports Centre, lack the glamour of the global arenas but modern international athletes owe a debt to Much Wenlock and its pioneering doctor.

Wenlock Edge in autumn.

A wooded way

▶ LINLEY TRACKWAY, SHROPSHIRE

The Linley Beeches in winter, south west of Linley Hall.

In the 17th century a mile-long avenue of oak trees was planted to create a grand approach for the Georgian stately home that is Linley Hall. However, high above the house, another avenue of trees stands out against the skyline, visible for miles in any direction. For years the double line of ancient beeches that stretch up Linley Hill were thought to have been planted by Napoleonic prisoners of war, but dendrochronology – tree-ring dating – has fixed the date at about 1740, around 80 years before England waged war with Napoleon's forces.

The reasons behind their planting are lost. They could be a marker to celebrate a battle or even in honour of a local wedding. They may just have sheltered the flocks of sheep that grazed the hillside. Most historians believe that they were planted by Robert More, MP for Shrewsbury and owner of the hall far below. A keen botanist, More had the earliest larch trees in England planted in his estate in the mid-18th century.

Unlike the avenue of oaks within the grounds of Linley Hall, the beeches don't follow a straight line. This has led some to believe that the trees were planted along the tracks of an ancient 6,000-year-old road. The trackway was probably a major route, running north–south across the Shropshire hills and may well have been used by the Romans linking the lead

How to get there:

Follow the signs for Linley on the A488 and take the road for The Bog and Cold Hill. As the road enters the wood you'll find a parking space next to the footpath for the Linley Beeches. For sat nav users: SY9 5HL (Linley Hall) Nearest railway station: Church Stretton (13 miles) Bus services: www.shropshirehillsshuttles. co.uk 0871 200 22 33

The Firs cottage in
Lower Broadheath,
the birthplace of
Sir Edward Elgar.

Other things to see:
The sweeping majesty of the
Malvern Hills proved to be an
inspiration for one of England's
finest composers, Sir Edward
Elgar. Visit his museum in the
village of Lower Broadheath
to discover more about the
landscapes that fuelled
his masterpieces.
For sat nav users: WR2 6RH
www.elgarmuseum.org
01905 333 224

Until this time the Malvern water industry continued to focus on Holy Well, although
that changed with the arrival of doctors James Wilson and James Manby Gully who opened
hydrotherapy centres based around the nearby St Anne's Well. The Water Cure was pricey but
popular, despite its unappealing regime. Treatment would begin at 6am sharp, when patients
would be packed in a sopping wet sheet and covered in blankets. An hour later they were
unwrapped and plunged into a descending douche to withstand 90 seconds of freezing cold
water poured over them from a height of 6 metres. Then, after a vigorous towelling down,
they were sent off on a bracing hike over the hills, stopping only to knock back 18 glasses
of water from various Malvern springs.

As no rich food, tobacco or alcohol were allowed, it is likely that the Cure's success
had more to do with a healthy diet and fresh air than the waters; after all, the Victorians
weren't known to eat well and hardly bathed. None the less, the rich and famous flocked
to take the waters, among them Charles Darwin, Florence Nightingale and Charles Dickens.
The latter thoughtfully dragged his wife here to endure constant cold showers after the birth
of their ninth child.

Long after the fashion for taking a cure dried up, Malvern waters continue to be held
in high regard. The Queen is reported to drink it every day and in December 2009 a new
bottling plant opened at the Holy Well site. The spring, housed in a restored Swiss-style
Victorian building, is open to the public every day free of charge between 9am and 4pm.

If you visit in May you'll also witness another age-old tradition: well-dressing. This entails
the locals decorating Holy Well and around thirty other sources in the area with flowers and
ribbons to give thanks for their miraculous properties.

The Blossom Trail
▶ THE VALE OF EVESHAM, WORCESTERSHIRE

Nestled between the Cotswolds and the Malvern Hills, the Vale of Evesham has been famous for its fruit since medieval times. Fertile soils and a sheltered climate make the area the second garden of England – after Kent. Originally the Vale was strewn with cider apple and pear orchards although the discovery of the Pershore Yellow Egg plum in Tiddesley Wood in 1827 brought soft-fruit production to Worcestershire and, by the 1870s, 900 tonnes of Pershore plums were being sent to market every year. The harvests were so great that local schools would close so that the children could pick the fruit with their mothers. In 1927, to celebrate the Yellow Egg's centenary, a steam train was christened the Pershore Plum, chugging between Worcester, Stratford-on-Avon and Birmingham. The train may have made its last journey but the legacy of the plum lives on. The Georgian town of Pershore still holds a Plum Fayre every August bank holiday with plum tastings and lashes of plum ale on the menu. Although the fruit-growing industry has slowed of late, there are still over 1,200 hectares (3,000 acres) of orchards in the Vale of Evesham that burst into colour between mid-March and mid-May. First comes the sweet aroma of damson flowers and white plum, closely followed by white pear and pink apple blossom a couple of weeks later.

The best way of enjoying this feast for the eyes is by taking the famous Blossom Trail, which has been walked, cycled and driven for over 25 years now. The circular waymarked route for cyclists starts at Evesham railway station. It has been specially designed to avoid as many right-hand turns as possible so that you don't have to worry about safety when taking in the sights and sounds of the hedgerows and orchards. And if walking or cycling the 40-mile trail sounds a little adventurous, coach trips leave from Evesham every day of the season, although it's obviously harder to enjoy the perfume of the blossom through all that glass.

How to get there:
Evesham is on the A4184 and the Blossom Trail starts at Evesham railway station. For sat nav users: WR11 4EQ
Bus services:
www.traveline.info
0871 200 22 33

Find out more:
www.worcestershires-heritage-garden.org
01386 446 944

Other things to see:
When Henry VIII sacked the monasteries the spectacular abbey at Evesham was demolished in 1539. However, we owe it to the locals, who managed to save the impressive bell tower, which still houses the peal of 40 bells and gives an idea of the sheer scale of what was the country's third-largest abbey. Find out more about the abbey and the history of Evesham at the nearby Almonry Museum. For sat nav users: WR11 4BG
www.almonryevesham.org
01386 446 944

The bell tower of Evesham Abbey, Abbey Park (left); cider trees in blossom along the Blossom Trail, Vale of Evesham (overleaf).

How to get there:
From the A1 take the A606 and follow the signs for Rutland Water. Use of the visitor centre is free but a small charge is made to enter the reserve.
For sat nav users: LE15 8RN
Nearest railway station: Oakham (4 miles)
Bus services:
www.pauljamescoaches.co.uk
01530 832 399

Find out more:
www.rutlandwater.org.uk
01572 770 651

Other things to see:
Rutland County Museum, in Oakham, opens up the history of the area. Admission, which is free, includes access to the Riding School, containing many original tools from traditional trades such as that of wheelwright, cooper and carpenter. It's also worth making the short walk to the Great Hall of Oakham Castle. Tradition stipulated that every visiting peer must give up one of his horse's shoes to the Lord of Oakham and so 200 hang from the castle walls.
For sat nav users: LE15 6HW
www.rutland.gov.uk
01572 758 440

After a couple of years, chicks will usually return to their place of birth to breed and the cycle will begin again. In 2006, the Rutland Osprey Project celebrated the return of the first naturally reared chick in central England for 150 years as a two-year-old male returned to the reservoir. Once established, ospreys mate for life, returning every year around March to their birthplace where they can be seen swooping down to the water to catch fish in their talons.

Of course, there's more to Rutland Water than ospreys. The nature reserve is home to over 250 species of birds, including goosanders, little ringed plovers, goldeneye and pintails while butterflies and dragonflies dart across the water. On 25 April 2009, birdwatcher Matthew Berriman spotted 109 different species of bird on the reserve, beating his previous record from eight years earlier. Could you do better?

Rutland Water viewed from the Anglian Water Bird Watching Centre at Egleton, Leicestershire.

Julia Bradbury's heart goes out to Rutland »

Every spring I get a pang to return home to Rutland. It's a heart-shaped county – the smallest in the land – smack bang in the middle of England. When you drive across its borders you're met with the motto *Multum in parvo* which means 'much in little'. How right that is. There's nothing like driving through the country lanes and seeing the shock of yellow in the fields as the rapeseed flowers bob in the wind. It's such an evocative image for me, taking me back to my childhood.

But where would I take you to show off this fantastic little county? We'd have to start at Burley-on-the-Hill house, which was built in the 1690s. The house itself is privately owned but you can visit the church of the Holy Cross in the grounds. From here we'd walk to the pretty village of Stamford with its bustling Friday market and then on to the Rutland Water reservoir, one of the best places in the country to ramble, sail or bird-watch. It's just perfect.

A geological puzzle
▶ PUZZLEWOOD, GLOUCESTERSHIRE

How to get there:

From Coleford take the
B4228 towards Chepstow
and follow brown tourist
signs for Puzzlewood.
For sat nav users: GL16 8QB
Nearest railway station:
Lydney (8 miles)
Bus services:
www.stagecoachbus.com
0871 200 22 33

Find out more:

www.puzzlewood.net
01594 833 187

Other things to see:

Were the forests of Middle Earth
inspired by the Forest of Dean
scowles? In 1929 the author
J. R. R. Tolkien was working on
the site of an archaeological dig
at Dwarf's Hill, a Roman temple
found in the Lydney Park
estate. At the time, the author
was developing *The Hobbit*
(1937) and some scholars
believe that the myths and
legends surrounding Dwarf's
Hill informed his fabled forests
of Mirkwood, Fangorn and
Lothlórien. Lydney Park Gardens
are open to the public in spring.
For sat nav users: GL15 6BU
www.lydneyparkestate.co.uk
01594 842 844

The lush Forest of Dean is peppered with a strange and at times downright spooky geological feature. Locally known as scowles, these rock formations are believed to exist only in this small corner of the planet.

The scowles were actually created naturally over millions of years, deep in the earth. The process began when cave systems formed in the carboniferous limestone beneath what is now the Forest of Dean. Over the centuries iron-rich mineral water filtered through the ground, finding its way into every nook and cranny in the rock, depositing iron ore in the process. After millennia of erosion and uplift, the cave system was exposed at the surface. The labyrinthine hollows were rich in iron ore and ready to be exploited by Iron Age settlers. The iron ore would have been removed from the scowles and prepared by crushing and roasting. It would then have been transferred to small, charcoal-fuelled furnaces, or bloomeries, for smelting. Once the iron was separated from the ore it could be fashioned into tools and weapons.

The exact date when mining began in Puzzlewood remains a mystery, but archaeologists have discovered ironwork from late prehistoric and Roman periods that share the same chemical signature as iron ores from the Forest of Dean. Coupled with the fact that a hoard of 3,000 Roman coins from the 3rd century AD was found by workmen in 1848 within the scowles at Puzzlewood, this discovery seems to indicate that mining had begun at least 2,000 years ago.

The scowles were only the beginning. When the early miners realised that they were tapping a rich seam of iron ore, they began to explore beneath the surface, excavating the caves that ran below the forest floor. However, when the Romans left they seemed to take with them any desire to mine the Forest of Dean and nature moved back to reclaim the scowles. Moss crept over the old workings and trees established themselves between the rocks, giving the landscape a unique, other-worldly appearance and the scowles descended into folklore and became the legendary homes of hobgoblins and dwarfs, places that invoked fear and trepidation.

Indeed, anyone with a fear of bats might still be wary of the scowles. The crags and surrounding oak, lime and beech trees make excellent homes for flying insects, which in turn makes Puzzlewood a feeding ground for several bat species including greater and lesser horseshoe and Bechstein's bats.

The spooky scowles
at Puzzlewood - the
home of magical
creatures perhaps?

Given the sack

❯ TETBURY, GLOUCESTERSHIRE

In medieval times Gumstool Hill in Tetbury was the local spot where witches and nagging wives were tormented. Since the 1970s, it has become the location for another form of torture as men, women and children charge up its steep incline, weighed down with a heavy bag of wool.

While sack races are a relatively modern invention, they probably do have some historical basis. Like much of Gloucestershire, Tetbury made its fortune with the wool trade. The Cotswold Lion, a shaggy, docile breed of sheep, dotted the hills with wool so strong and lustrous that it became known as the golden fleece. The wealth it raised helped build the region's monasteries and cathedrals and, on a national scale, funded wars. Such was its value that when the crusader Richard the Lionheart was taken prisoner in Austria, his ransom was set as 50,000 sacks of English wool. Even today, the Lord Chancellor sits on a sack stuffed with wool in the House of Lords, a sign of how important the humble sheep was to the fortunes of the kingdom.

In the 17th century young drovers, stopping in Tetbury on their epic journeys to market, would prove their virility to the local wenches by hauling a pack of wool on to their back and racing up the steep incline of Gumstool Hill. The tradition died out along with the wool trade until in 1973 it was revived as part of the Tetbury Festival. Since then, every May (Woolsack Day usually falls on the Whitsun bank holiday), competitors have lugged a 27-kg sack of wool up the 252-metre incline between the Royal Oak and the Crown Inn. If that sounds backbreaking enough, consider that the gradient of Gumstool Hill is 1 in 4. The sack, custom-made by the British Wool Federation, is slung across the competitors' back and shoulders, allowing them to keep a tight hold on the two front corners. In these times of equal opportunities a female heat has been added, although the ladies do get to carry a lighter load of 16kg.

In 1999 the course was shortened from 252 metres to 219 metres but as Tom Heap attested when he ran the race for *Countryfile* in 2007, even this is quite a feat. Tom didn't do too badly, finishing third in his heat.

How to get there:
Tetbury is on the A433 and the Royal Oak pub is at 1 Cirencester Road. For sat nav users: GL8 8EY Nearest railway station: Kemble (6 miles). Bus services: www.traveline.info 0871 200 22 33

Find out more:
www.tetburywoolsack.co.uk 01666 503 552

Other things to see:
Tetbury itself is a haven for antique lovers with over 25 shops in which to mooch around. The town centre is dominated by its pillared market house, originally built in 1655 to store and sell that all-important wool.

Woolsack racers run up the steep incline to the race finish at the Crown Inn.

White gold

▶ COLESBOURNE PARK, GLOUCESTERSHIRE

How to get there:

Colesbourne Park is located
halfway between Cheltenham
and Cirencester, directly
off the A435.
For sat nav users: GL53 9NP
Nearest railway station:
Cheltenham Spa (9 miles)
Bus services:
www.stagecoachbus.com
0871 200 22 33

Find out more:

www.snowdrop.org.uk
01242 870 264

There is perhaps nothing more heartening than seeing the first snowdrops poking through the frosty ground of late January, signalling that winter is waning and spring is around the corner. The prolific *Galanthus* is found all across Britain, but is not native. No one really knows how it reached British soil although the sheer quantities found around monasteries, abbeys and churches suggest that holy men brought them back from their journeys to Italy.

The first reference to the humble snowdrop is found in herbalist John Gerarde's *The Herball or Generall Historie of Plantes* (1597) and now 20 wild species exist, spread out from their heartland in Turkey all across Europe, with a staggering 700 cultivated varieties on offer.

Such passion would have been recognised by Victorian naturalist Henry John Elwes, who in the late 19th century established the world's largest collection of snowdrop bulbs at Colesbourne Park, near Cheltenham. In 1874 Elwes was travelling in western Turkey where he discovered what became one of Britain's best-loved snowdrops, one that still bears his name to this day: *Galanthus elwesii*.

After Elwes' death the gardens fell into neglect and by the time the present Henry Elwes inherited the estate in 1956, the mansion had suffered the same fate. Faced with the prospect of refurbishing a ruin, Henry pulled it down two years later, building a new house that incorporated rooms from the old mansion. The snowdrops themselves were rediscovered some 30 years ago and in 2003 work began to restore the gardens under the guidance of Dr John Grimshaw, one of Britain's foremost authorities on the snowdrop. Each weekend in February the private gardens open for everyone to enjoy the 250 varieties of snowdrop that continue to spread across the huge banks of the lake and in cultivated displays through the arboretum. Alongside the snow-white banks, masses of daffodils, tulips and hellebores bring Colesbourne's 4 hectares (10 acres) to life later in the spring.

Other things to see:

In the shadow of a more famous near-neighbour,
Westonbirt, is a Cotswolds 'secret garden', 27 miles
from Colesbourne, and it's well worth seeking out.
Batsford Arboretum's 20 hectares (50 acres) are a
delight, housing flowering cherries and magnolias
in spring, sorbus and maples in autumn. The
garden is influenced by Chinese and Japanese
landscapes with stands of bamboo and numerous
sculptures beneath the boughs.
For sat nav users: GL56 9AB
www.batsarb.co.uk
01386 701 441

Snowdrops at
Colesbourne Park.

The house where time stands still

> ## CALKE ABBEY, DERBYSHIRE

How to get there:

Calke Abbey is located at
Ticknall on the A514 between
Swadlincote and Melbourne.
For sat nav users: DE73 7LE
Nearest railway station:
Derby (9½ miles)
Bus services:
www.arrivabus.co.uk
0871 200 22 33

Find out more:

www.nationaltrust.org.uk/
main/w-calkeabbey
01332 863 822

Other things to see:

As with most National Trust
properties, the house is only
half the story. The 80 hectares
(198 acres) of the 240-hectare
(593-acre) grounds of Calke
Abbey are a National Nature
Reserve, largely due to its
collection of veteran trees that
were planted over 300 years
ago. The real survivors are
some of the 200 huge oaks that
dominate the gardens, two of
which are over 1,000 years old.

The Bird Lobby at
Calke Abbey.

Calke Abbey is a veritable Aladdin's cave of discovery. Rebuilt in 1704, the house was acquired
by the National Trust in 1985. It had previously been owned by the Hapur-Crewes, a family of
reclusive eccentrics who hoarded everything they laid their hands on. Badly needing repair
and lacking in most modern amenities, the place was rammed with clutter accumulated by
generations of Harpur-Crewes over almost 360 years.

The National Trust made a somewhat unusual decision to carry out the repairs but leave
the contents of the house exactly how they were found. Time has stood still ever since, a
perfect illustration of the great English house in decline and a place where, quite literally, you
never know what you'll find around every corner. Keep your eye out for the crocodile skull
brought back from Egypt or the perhaps most bizarre christening present ever given –
a knick-knack fashioned from boars' tusks and a silver-mounted ostrich egg.

The greatest discovery was an early 18th-century state bed with intricate Chinese silk
hangings, seemingly unpacked and kept in its wrapping as it was too tall for the intended
bedroom (it has now been assembled).

Keeping the house in such a state takes effort and every year before the spring opening
the housekeeping team sets about cleaning the esoteric collection. The walls of the abbey

are covered with hunting trophies. Each is spruced up using vaccum cleaners and soft brushes by staff wearing rubber gloves and masks. And if you think the protective clothing is for the trophies, think again – most of the taxidermy is preserved in arsenic.

As you might expect at Calke, not everything goes exactly to plan. One year, when replacing Elizabethan drains, workmen were shocked to find human skulls grinning up at them. The house itself is built on the remains of an old priory – hence the suitably unusual name – and an old monk's burial site had been uncovered. The skeletons were left where they were and new drains installed in a different location. All in a day's work for staff at one of Britain's most idiosyncratic houses.

The Haxey Hood

❯ HAXEY, LINCOLNSHIRE

Twelfth Night may not be the national celebration it once was but for the usually peaceful village of Haxey it's one day that never goes unmarked. Every year on 6 January the young men of the village go head to head with their rivals in nearby Westwoodside in one of the biggest rugby scrums in the country.

The day of madness and mud began in the 14th century when the daughter of a local landowner, Lady de Mowbray, was returning home from chapel. A gust of wind blew her red silk hood from her head and, in order to please their squire, 13 labourers tumbled after it.

How to get there:
Leave the M180 at Junction 2 and take the A161 to Haxey. The King's Arms is in Low Street. For sat nav users: DN9 2LA
Nearest railway station: Gainsborough Central (7 miles)
Bus services:
www.traveline.info
0871 200 22 33

Find out more:
www.visitnorthlincolnshire.com
01652 657 053

The 'fool of Haxey' gives the traditional speech at the start of the Haxey Hood games.

Finally one lad managed to catch the wayward hood but, too bashful to return it in person, handed it to a mate to lay at her ladyship's feet.

The shenanigans of these workmen so amused Lady de Mowbray that she granted her heroes a patch of land, known forever more as the Hoodlands. The only stipulation was that they reenacted the event every year. Before she left she christened her hood's shy saviour the 'fool of Haxey' and his gallant accomplice 'the Lord of the game'.

Fast-forward 700 years and elements of this suspiciously tall tale are all more or less still there. No longer silk, the Hood is now a piece of rope bound in leather presided over by 13 officials or Boggans. One is selected as the fool, blacked up and dressed in rags, while the Lord, wearing top hat and hunting jacket, becomes the master of ceremonies.

Before the game begins, the Fool makes the traditional speech: 'Hoos agen hoos, toon agen toon if tha meets a man nok im doon, but doant 'ot im' (or, should you need it: 'House against house, town against town, if you meet a man, knock him down but don't hurt him.') Just to make things a little more uncomfortable for the poor soul, his fellow Boggans set light to a bale of straw behind the Fool, enshrouding him in choking smoke.

The titanic tussle begins when the hood is thrown into the air and the individual who catches it suddenly finds himself faced with some 300 men, all trying to get the prize back either to the King's Arms pub in Haxey or the Carpenter's Arms in Westwoodside. The game – a health-and-safety officer's nightmare if there ever were one – can easily roll on for three or four hours before the hood makes it into the hands of one of the respective landlords. The cheer goes up, the hood is anointed with ale and placed on display until the following year. Then the real drinking begins.

Other things to see:
After the rough and tumble of the Haxey Hood, where better to calm the nerves than the nearby village of Epworth, the birthplace of John and Charles Wesley, founders of Methodism? Visit the Old Rectory, the Wesley family home, or stand where John Wesley delivered some of his most rousing sermons.
For sat nav users: DN9 1HX
www.epwortholdrectory.org.uk
01427 872 268

Bronze statue of John
Wesley at Epsworth.

A new home for wildlife
❯ FRAMPTON MARSH, LINCOLNSHIRE

The RSPB has operated a nature reserve at Frampton since 1984 but until recently it was quite a low-key site. Then in 2007 the reserve's neighbours upped sticks and moved to the United States giving the charity the chance to buy the land. The arable farmland had once been part of a much larger Wash that stretched from Lincoln to Peterborough, Britain's equivalent of the Everglades in Florida. Investment and expansion began and two years and £1.6 million later the new-look Frampton Marsh reserve opened to the public.

One of the first tasks was to raise South Lincolnshire's largest reedbed to act as a store for water through the summer months for the wetland habitat. Over a period of three months, 90 volunteers and RSPB staff planted 15,000 reed seedlings, covering 5 per cent of the reserve's 20-hectare (50-acre) reservoir. Other habitats include three 7-hectare (17-acre) 'scrapes' – areas of shallow water – up to 40 centimetres in depth. Each scrape features a series of islands topped with sand, cockles or shingle that are full of invertebrates and annual weeds, providing freshwater feasts for wading birds and ducks. Creating the scrapes was a precision job using bulldozers fitted with laser technology to ensure the depth of water was just right. The habitats certainly seem to have suited the avocets and little ringed plovers that nested here in the first few seasons.

The improved reserve has proved a hit with both wildfowl and an annual 35,000 human visitors; and the freshwater habitats of the 565-hectare (1,396-acre) reserve are fast becoming favourites with birdwatchers.

Other things to see:

The Frampton Marsh 360 hides offer, as the name suggests, a 360-degree view of the new reserve, bringing the wildlife of the Wash closer to an appreciative audience. Admission is free.

How to get there:

Frampton Marsh is signposted on the A16 Boston to Kirton road.

Nearest railway station: Boston (4 miles)

Bus services: www.kimesbuses.co.uk 01529 497 251

Find out more:

www.rspb.org.uk/ framptonmarsh 01205 724 678

A wading avocet, a frequent visitor to Frampton Marsh.

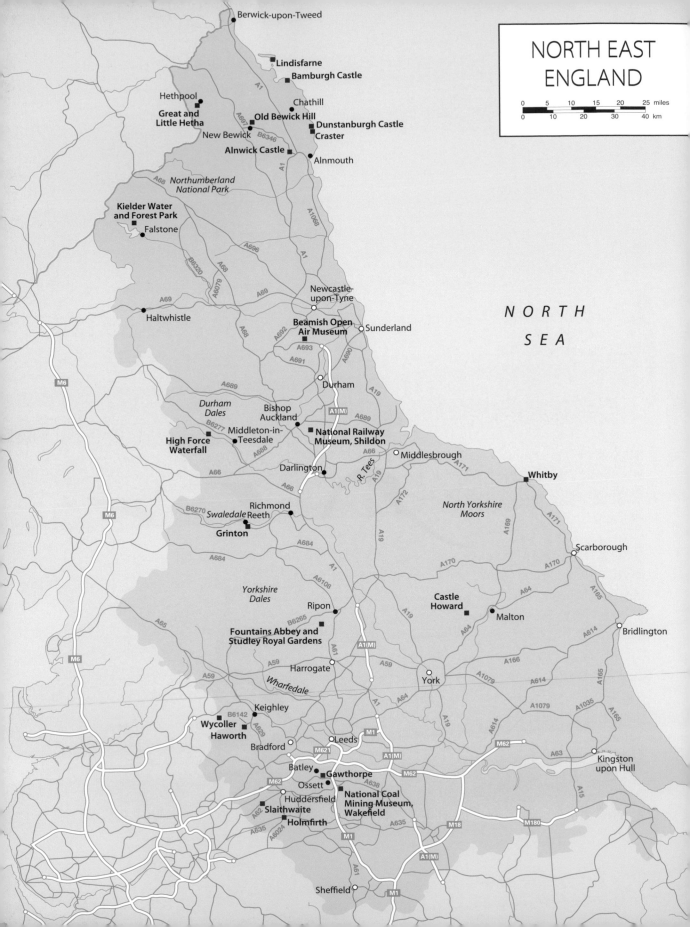

NORTH EAST ENGLAND

0 5 10 15 20 25 miles
0 10 20 30 40 km

Berwick-upon-Tweed

Lindisfarne
Bamburgh Castle

Hethpool
Great and
Little Hetha
Old Bewick Hill
Chathill

Dunstanburgh Castle
Craster

New Bewick

Alnwick Castle
Alnmouth

Northumberland
National Park

Kielder Water
and Forest Park
Falstone

Haltwhistle

Newcastle-
upon-Tyne

Beamish Open
Air Museum
Sunderland

Durham

Durham
Dales
Bishop
Auckland
Middleton-in-
Teesdale
High Force
Waterfall

National Railway
Museum, Shildon

Darlington
R. Tees
Middlesbrough

Whitby

Richmond
Reeth
Swaledale
Grinton

North Yorkshire
Moors

Scarborough

Yorkshire
Dales
Ripon

Castle
Howard
Malton

Fountains Abbey and
Studley Royal Gardens

Bridlington

Harrogate

York

Wharfedale

Keighley

Wycoller
Haworth

Bradford
Leeds

Kingston
upon Hull

Batley
Gawthorpe
Ossett
Huddersfield
Slaithwaite
Holmfirth

National Coal
Mining Museum,
Wakefield

Sheffield

NORTH
SEA

North East

The countryside is much more than views and scenery, although the North East has more than its fair share of spectacle. But it's the people who work the landscape who have made our countryside great – and always will. It's all too easy to remember the rich and powerful, as the religious houses of Lindisfarne and Fountains Abbey to the impressive stately homes of Alnwick and Castle Howard bear witness. However, throughout history it was the hard work of ordinary folk, striving day in and day out, that forged the landscape we now mistakenly think of as natural. Too often, the only monuments to their tireless endeavours are abandoned buildings such as the evocative stone barns of Swaledale. Thankfully the times are a-changing and attractions, such as the Beamish Open Air Museum, open our eyes to what life was like in the years gone by, letting us step quite literally into history.

Of course, we still manipulate the countryside to this day, adapting it to suit our purpose. You have to wonder if, in years to come, people will look back at reservoirs such as Kielder Water and marvel at how our generation changed the face of the countryside for ever.

Britain's biggest treehouse
▶ ALNWICK GARDEN, NORTHUMBERLAND

How to get there:

Alnwick Castle and Garden are just off the A1. The castle is open Mar–Oct but the Garden opens in winter too.

For sat nav users: NE66 1YU

Nearest railway station: Alnmouth (4 miles)

Bus services:

www.traveline.org.uk

0871 200 22 33

Find out more:

www.alnwickgarden.com

01665 511 350

Stone barns near Gunnerside (previous page); the Lion Bridge at Alnwick Castle (below); Alnwick's treehouse (opposite).

Alnwick Castle is one of Northumberland's most striking landmarks. Often called the Windsor of the North, it's England's second-largest inhabited castle. Originally built in the early 1300s as a medieval fortress, the castle has been home to the Percys, earls and dukes of Northumberland, for seven centuries. It is also a regular sight on both the big and small screen, having doubled for Harry Potter's Hogwarts, Edmund Blackadder's castle and even the lair of Count Dracula.

The last 15 years have seen the garden of Alnwick undergo a transformation of almost cinematic proportions. When the current Duchess of Northumberland, Jane Percy, was given some land to develop by her husband in 1996, it was overgrown, unsightly and had been set to be covered in tarmac to create a car park. Thanks to the Duchess's vision for creating a new garden attraction for the North and a £45 million budget, the results are spectacular. It now boasts ornamental gardens, a bamboo labyrinth, an interactive water sculpture, and a pond that is frozen for six months of the year for ice-skating.

After reading from a survey that one-third of children in Britain aren't allowed to climb trees anymore, the Duchess wanted to provide a place where kids could experience what it's like to be up in the treetops safely. The Alnwick treehouse is a higgledy-piggledy child's fantasy constructed from sustainable Scandinavian redwood, Canadian cedar and English and Scots pine. The entire structure has been designed in such a way that the trees can continue to grow unperturbed by the treehouse. And it's not only children who can enjoy its restaurant, story rooms and roaring open fire. Connected by a series of ramps and wobbly wooden bridges the treehouse is almost entirely accessible by buggy and wheelchair.

Other things to see:

Back on the ground, the gardens offer another killer attraction – the Poison Garden, which you can only visit accompanied by a guide and which contains 90 deadly species of plant. The castle is a separate attraction but well worth a visit too, if you have enough time after exploring the gardens. From Renaissance paintings and porcelain to family-friendly attractions such as the Knight's Quest and Harry Potter-themed tours, there is plenty to see and do.

www.alnwickcastle.com

01665 510 777

Matt Baker makes himself at home in the castle »

To celebrate Bonfire Night we visited Alnwick Castle, best known these days as one of the locations of the Harry Potter films. Back in 1605, it was the home of Sir Thomas Percy, one of the five principal conspirators in the Gunpowder Plot to blow up the Houses of Parliament.

Castles often feel cold and austere, more a museum than a place where people lived. That couldn't be further from the truth at Alnwick. It's still the home of the Duke and Duchess of Northumberland and has a real lived-in feeling, so intimate and welcoming. I remember wandering into one of the libraries and thinking it's the kind of place you can imagine kicking off your shoes and diving into a good book.

Lewisburn Bay at Kielder Water and Forest Park.

previously inaccessible areas. If you get tired after your walk, you can also pop on to the ferries that take you across the water.

The man-made lake itself was created to service Teesside's booming industry and was officially opened by HM Queen Elizabeth II in 1982. Unfortunately, the boom soon turned to bust and Kielder Water became an embarrassment as one factory after another closed down in the area. However, since then the reservoir and its surrounding 150 million planted trees have been appreciated as an important habitat for local wildlife, unique art installations and a fantastic place to explore or enjoy nature.

The bird hide in the Bakethin Conservation Area is ideal for watching cormorants, wading birds and even otters at daybreak and dusk. However, for one of the best chances you'll ever have of spotting a native red squirrel, head to the hide at Leaplish Waterside Park. Kielder Forest is home to around 70 per cent of England's entire red-squirrel population, thanks to its dense conifers, which grey squirrels find difficult to colonise. You have to wonder what the squirrels make of some of the modern art.

Find out more:
www.visitkielder.com
01434 220 616

John Craven on the Northumberland Coast »

The Northumberland Coast is 60 miles of fantastic scenery. Of course, everyone knows Bamburgh Castle and Holy Island but that's only the beginning of the story. There's the ruin of Dunstanburgh Castle and the fishing village of Craster, famous for its delicious kippers. Then there's mile upon mile of bleak, wild landscapes. At certain times of the year you can walk on a beach and never see another person.

They say that Northumberland is Britain's best-kept secret. I think a lot of us are trying to change that these days.

The lack of light pollution makes Kielder a star-gazer's paradise and the new observatory and planetarium in the heart of the forest offers unparalleled views of the heavens.

The giant head of 'Silvas Capitalis', created by American artists SIMPARCH.

A holy orchid

❭ LINDISFARNE, NORTHUMBERLAND

How to get there:
Leave the A1 northbound
at Berwick-upon-Tweed,
continuing on to the
Lindisfarne Causeway. Check
the tide times before travelling.
For sat nav users: TD15 2SH
Nearest railway station:
Berwick-upon-Tweed (10 miles)
Bus services:
www.travelsure.co.uk
01665 720 955

Find out more:
www.visitnorthumberland.com
01289 330 733

Until 1082, England's most north-easterly land mass was known by the Anglo-Saxon word Lindisfarne. The arrival of Saint Aidan in the 7th century prompted the building of the first wooden monastery on the island in AD 635. Over a century and a half later, in 793, the island came under a vicious and bloody Viking attack and when Benedictine monks rebuilt the priory in 1082 it was renamed Holy Island in honour of the martyrs and soon became a pilgrim destination.

Modern visitors making the 3-mile journey across the mudflats to Lindisfarne are just as likely to be birdwatchers because, at low tide, the causeway is alive with wading birds including godwits, dunlin, knot and wigeon while the island's inner harbour attracts oyster catchers, grebes and red-throated divers.

The village and ruins of
the 11th-century priory.
If you get caught out by
the tide or simply want
to stay a little longer, the
village as a number of
friendly pubs and cosy
bed and breakfasts to
shelter in.

More recently, the eyes of wildlife-watchers have turned towards to the sand-dunes. Look carefully among the western dunes and you could be lucky enough to find the Lindisfarne Helleborine orchid. While this unassuming flower has long been acknowledged as rare, recent DNA testing has revealed that the plant – *Epipactis sancta*, to give it its scientific name – is a species in its own right. With only 300 or so found on the island its status has now been elevated as it is one of the rarest orchids on the planet.

It's fair to say that it isn't the showiest of plants. With yellow-green petals and stiff light green leaves, the orchid can grow up to 60cm tall. But if you come across one, you're looking at a plant that grows nowhere else on earth.

One plant that isn't so welcome on the Holy Island is pirri-pirri-bur, a type of burr that originates in New Zealand. This hardy plant is believed to have been transported to Scotland in shipments of wool and it then floated down the River Tweed. There are fears that if it takes hold it will stabilise the shifting sands of the dunes, altering the habitat in which the Lindisfarne orchid has its precarious hold. The burrs stick to anything and some dog owners have had to shave their pets to rid their coats of the troublesome burrs.

This isn't to say that dog-lovers should deny themselves the beauty of the island and its flora and fauna. It just pays to keep to the paths and not allow dogs to range in the dunes in the summer months.

Other things to see:

Lindisfarne Castle was built in 1570 from stone from the ruined priory as part of the war effort against Scotland. By 1901, when the founder of *Country Life* magazine, Edward Hudson, discovered it, the castle was in a sorry state. He transformed it into a holiday home, now maintained by the National Trust.
www.nationaltrust.org.uk/
lindisfarne
01289 389 244

Lindisfarne Castle
viewed from the Priory.

Matt Baker goes back to his roots »

For me, the Durham Dales are a classic case of not knowing how brilliant a place is until you leave it. It was a real privilege to go back to where I was born and show *Countryfile* viewers where I grew up.

And what better way than finding out that my childhood home is slap bang in the middle of one of the most peaceful places in Britain? I couldn't believe it when the researchers from Northumbria University rolled out their map. There was our family farm right in the centre of the country's top spot for tranquillity. I'd always known it was special but now it's been scientifically proven.

The mighty High
Force waterfall.

Tranquillity and tumult
〉 THE DURHAM DALES, DURHAM

How to get there:

The nearest major road is the A66. Follow the signs for High Force, at the Upper Teesdale Raby Estate, on the B6277, near Middleton-in-Teesdale. Open access all year round.

For sat nav users: DL12 0QG
Nearest railway station:
Bishop Auckland (20 miles)
There is no bus service.

Covering around one-third of the county of Durham, the Durham Dales area encompasses both Weardale and Teesdale and is characterised by open moorland, sweeping meadows and heather-clad hills. Is it any wonder it has been named Britain's most tranquil spot?

In 2006, researchers from Northumberland university set out to map and test the tranquillity of the British countryside. They surveyed 500 countryside users to distil just what people meant by tranquillity. Those questioned talked about seeing rolling natural landscapes, running water and woodland or experiencing peace and quiet, broken only by the sounds of nature, such as birdsong. When quizzed about the opposite of tranquillity people cited light pollution, the constant noise of traffic or aircraft and the presence of crowds. None of these is a problem in the Durham Dales – striding over the remote moorland, the only sound you're likely to hear is the wind rustling through the heather.

One of the Dales' more noisy attractions is the High Force waterfall. It's England's highest uninterrupted drop of water, where the River Tees plunges 21 metres into a churning pool and it is anything but quiet as the noise and drama of the waterfall is breathtaking. The falls are also a real snapshot of Britain's geological past. The lower part of the gorge is made up of limestone, sandstone and shale, deposited in eras when the now serene Dales were variously the bed of a long-vanished ocean, parched desert and tropical rainforest. Then, 295 million years ago, molten rock injected up through the limestone, spreading out to form the hard lip known as Whin Sill – the same ridge that carries Hadrian's Wall in Northumberland. The land was subsequently buried under vast ice sheets that gouged and sculpted the rugged layers that the River Tees continues to plummet over in the 21st century.

From the moment you hear the muffled thunder of the falls at the start of the woodland walk down to the gorge to when you first experience that near-deafening roar up close, High Force commands your respect and awe.

Find out more:
www.visitcountydurham.com
01833 640 209

Other things to see:
The world's first passenger train left Shildon station in 1825. Today the oldest railway town in the country is home to the National Railway Museum, a free attraction with over 100 locomotives to view. For sat nav users: DL4 1PQ
www.nrm.org.uk
01388 777 999

Living history
› BEAMISH OPEN AIR MUSEUM, COUNTY DURHAM

Unless you can knock up a TARDIS in your back shed, Beamish Open Air Museum is the nearest you'll get to time travel. Don't expect dusty artefacts safely tucked behind glass or roped off in stuffy rooms. Spread out across 121 hectares (300 acres) of woodland, this is a living, breathing reconstruction of northern country life in the 18th and 19th centuries.

How to get there:
Take the A1(M) to Junction 63, following the signs on the A693.
For sat nav users: DH9 0RG
Nearest railway station: Newcastle Upon Tyne (15 miles)
Bus services:
www.travelinenortheast.info
0871 200 22 33

The tram travelling through The Town – modelled on pre-First World War Britain, at Beamish Open Air Museum.

The 19th-century
Co-operative store
found in The Town.

Other things to see:

One thing that didn't have to
be moved to Beamish was the
Mahogany Drift Mine, which
opened on this site in 1855.
Collect your lamp, pop on a
hard hat and descend to the
bowels of the earth, thanking
your lucky stars that you don't
have to work in these kind of
conditions every day.

Find out more:

www.beamish.org.uk
0191 370 4000

Not many museums offer you the chance to wander around a market town that is
straight out of the 1820s. Jump on the trams that rattle and shake along the cobbled streets
and take in the Victorian splendour of Ravensworth Terrace, seeing how the other half
used to live. You'll be amazed at how realistic the street looks and for good reason. Beamish
isn't a modern interpretation of the past, it literally is the past, transported brick by brick
from different locations around the county. Ravensworth, for example, originally stood in
Gateshead and was rebuilt from scratch in its new location, a painstaking labour of love –
likewise the grand Masonic Hall, which was relocated from Sunderland, and even Westoe
Netty, a men's urinal constructed in South Shields in 1890. As you head on to the high street,
make sure you check out the Co-op packed with products from the 1870s, give your sweet
tooth a treat at the Jubilee Sweet Factory, and even pop your head around the strong-room
vault of the local bank. If all that has worked up a thirst, then no visit to Beamish is complete
without a visit to the Sun Inn. The sawdust-strewn pub originally served the working men of
Bishop Auckland in County Durham and is fully licensed to sell local ales.

Everywhere you go there are staff in authentic period costumes, always ready to spin
you a yarn or explain what you're seeing. Did you know, for example, that Victorians quite
often bought second-hand teeth from the dentist? Outside of the town, is Home Farm where
you get acquainted with the now rare breeds that would have kept farmers busy, while the
colliery village gives you a fascinating insight to life down and around the pit. No journey
into history is complete without a trip on a steam train. The Pockerley Waggonway is an
1825 engine shed, the only place in Beamish where you'll find replicas, and copies of George
Stephenson's Locomotion No. 1, Puffing Billy and the Steam Elephant roar along the line in
the valley below the manor house.

Spend a day at Beamish and there's every chance you'll find it hard to return to the
21st century.

Saved by schoolgirls
❯ CASTLE HOWARD, NORTH YORKSHIRE

During the Second World War the grand surroundings of Castle Howard were home to the girls of Queen Margaret's School in Escrick, who had been sent inland to escape coastal bombing campaigns. Tragedy struck on 9 November 1940 when the music mistress awoke at 5am and smelt smoke. She discovered the fire that would sweep through the south-east wing of the house, destroying 20 rooms and bringing down the house's famous 21-metre high dome. Priceless Chippendale furniture and Canaletto paintings were lost to the flames,

Atlas Fountain and Castle Howard.

but countless works of art were saved by the pupils themselves. As the domestic-science teacher frantically pedalled on her push bike to raise the alarm the six-formers ran into the inferno and grabbed paintings off the walls to save the canvases. You can still see the scars on the Great Hall's marble floor, burnt by gobbets of molten lead dropping from the dome high above.

Castle Howard's future was only secured by George Howard who returned from the war to inherit the property in 1946 after the death in action of his two brothers. Its condition was so poor that the trustees had started to sell its treasures, convinced it was becoming uninhabitable. George thought differently and began a programme of restoration that led to Castle Howard becoming, in 1952, one of the first private stately homes to open to the public. Ten years later the house was crowned once again with a restored dome and as recently as 2009 the High South apartments were re-opened.

It's easy to see why 217,000 people walk through the doors of Castle Howard every year. Instantly recognisable as the location for both the television and cinematic versions of Evelyn Waugh's *Brideshead Revisited*, the house was designed by Sir John Vanbrugh in 1699 for his friend Charles Howard, the 3rd Earl of Carlisle. As Vanbrugh had no architectural experience he turned to Nicholas Hawksmoor, who had worked with Sir Christopher Wren, to draw up plans. Such was the ambition of the final design that the house took over a century to complete, by which time the Earl and Vanbrugh were both long dead.

The ongoing restoration and maintenance of Castle Howard is a monumental task. The estate covers 4,047 hectares (10,000 acres) made up of more than 400 hectares (1,000 acres) of formal gardens, over 800 hectares (2,000 acres) of managed woodland and 2,428 hectares (6,000 acres) of farmland. The house itself is so large that even its roof is measured in acres. To think such splendour could have been lost for ever were it not for the quick action of a bunch of schoolgirls and their teachers.

How to get there:

Castle Howard is found just off the A64 northbound. For sat nav users: YO60 7DA Nearest railway station: Malton (7½ miles) Bus services: www.yorkshiretravel.net 0871 200 22 33

Find out more:

www.castlehoward.co.uk 01653 648 333

The interior corridor gallery of Roman sculptures at Castle Howard (opposite); Castle Howard Mausoleum and New River Bridge (below).

Other things to see:

The spectacular mausoleum, standing a mile from the house, was intended as the last resting place of the 3rd Earl of Carlisle. Work began in 1729 and took 12 years to complete. Unfortunately by that time the Earl had already died and was buried in the local parish church. His body was duly disinterred and returned to Castle Howard, to the mausoleum that has become the final resting place of his family ever since. There are a handful of pre-booked tours available with the curator each year. Alternatively, you can view the mausoleum from the house and gardens of Castle Howard.

Water wonders

▶ FOUNTAINS ABBEY AND STUDLEY ROYAL WATER GARDEN, NORTH YORKSHIRE

How to get there:

Fountains Abbey is signposted from the A1 and is located 4 miles west of Ripon off the B6265.

For sat nav users: HG4 3DY

Nearest railway station: Harrogate (10 miles)

Bus services:
www.littleredbus.co.uk
01423 526 655

The vaulted ceilings of the cellarium at Fountains Abbey.

Britain's largest monastic ruin, the spellbinding Fountains Abbey, began life in 1132 as the humble home of Benedictine monks. The land had been given to the holy men by the Archbishop of York and was a wild place described in reports of the time as: 'fit rather to the lair of wild beasts than the home of human beings.' However, when the same monks were admitted into the Cistercian Order three years later, Fountains was transformed into one of the most powerful, and richest, religious communities in all of England – at least until Henry VIII got his hands on it.

In Cistercian orders, lay brothers relieved the monks from day-to-day chores. At Fountains they seemed to go into overdrive. The Abbey soon became a hive of industry with iron working, lead mining, horse breeding, and it maintained impressive flocks of sheep. The results are still to be seen today in the remarkable 51-metre church tower and the arched cellarium that spans over 90 metres and somehow managed to survive the Dissolution of the Monasteries. As you look up admiringly at the vaulted ceiling under which the lay brothers would have eaten and socialised, keep an eye out for the eight species of bat, including Daubenton's and soprano pipistrelle, that now make the Abbey their home.

Find out more:

www.fountainsabbey.org.uk

01765 608 888

Temple of Piety
seen across the
water at Studley
Royal Water Gardens.

Another survivor of Henry's dissolution was the Abbey's watermill, which was spared destruction in 1539 as it was able to generate the princely sum of £3 a year for subsequent owners. Today you can try your hand at milling corn with the same grinding materials utilised throughout its 850-year history.

Those sections of the Abbey that were razed to the ground didn't go to waste. Glass and lead found their way to Ripon and York and much of the stone from the ruin was used to build the impressive Fountains Hall, built during the golden age of Elizabeth I's reign.

In 1767 the Fountains estate was purchased by William Aislabie of neighbouring Studley Royal. William landscaped the already beautiful estates into what is now one of the most significant examples of an 18th-century water garden. Scattered with mesmerising follies, temples and statues, the garden was designed to surprise and amuse at every turn. At any time of year the result of the Aislabie endeavours is truly spellbinding, framed by the dramatic cliffs of the Skell Valley, a jewel in the crown of the National Trust which was bequeathed the Abbey and Water Garden in 1983.

Other things to see:

Owned by English Heritage and managed by the National Trust, St Mary's church, nestled in the Fountains estate, was consecrated in 1878 despite its mock-Gothic architecture. Keep an eye out for carved multi-coloured parrots – a favourite of architect William Burges – that perch above the choir stalls. Open from Easter–end of Sept.

How to get there:
From the M6, take Junction 40
for the A66 east, then follow the
signs for Richmond, picking up
the B6270 for Reeth.
Nearest railway stations:
Garsdale, Dent or Kirkby
Stephen
Bus services:
www.littleredbus.co.uk
01423 526 655

Find out more:
www.yorkshiredales.org.uk
01748 884 059

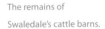

The remains of
Swaledale's cattle barns.

Summer meadows
❯ SWALEDALE, NORTH YORKSHIRE

James Alfred Wright, better known as writer James Herriot, once wrote of Swaledale: 'This
high country is too bleak for some people, but it is up there on the empty moors, with the
curlews crying, that I have been able to find peace and tranquillity. It is a land of pure air,
rocky streams and hidden waterfalls.'

Swaledale has to be one of the most undeveloped areas in the country when it comes
to tourism, but that's not something that worries the people who have discovered this
wonderfully secluded corner of Yorkshire. In winter the rolling dales are, as you'd expect, bleak
and not for the faint-hearted, but return in early summer and you'll be in for a treat. Enter
the valleys by either the Pennine Way or Alfred Wainwright's Coast to Coast Walk (two great
walking routes that cross in pretty Keld) and you'll be met by a carpet of yellow. Look closer
and you'll see buttercups of course, but also a dazzling array of wild flowers and plants.

Other things to see:

St Andrew's church in Grinton was once the largest parish in all of England, serving a 20-mile radius of the Dales. Nicknamed the Cathedral of the Dales, villagers had often to brave a dangerous 16-mile journey in hazardous conditions to take their dead to be buried in Grinton. Eventually another church was built at Muker so the so-called Corpse Way fell out of use. In a somewhat lighter vein, the same route is used today by walkers enjoying the countryside between Keld and Grinton.

Red fescue, pignut, bustort and sweet vernal-grass crowd the meadows, undisturbed by man or beast. Every May, Swaledale farmers move their livestock out of the meadows, leaving the lush, green pastures to bloom, ready for hay later in the year. While its riches are already manifold, Swaledale is also benefiting from the Yorkshire Dales Hay Time project, which is gathering the seed from existing bountiful meadows to help restore 80 hectares (nearly 200 acres) of upland and 60 hectares (some 150 acres) of lowland Dales to their former species-rich grassland cover. It's a long process but one that will ensure that the timeless scenes that greet you in Swaledale survive beyond old photographs.

Sadly some aspects of Swaledale life have come and gone. The multitude of squat, stone barns that once over-wintered cattle lie, in the main, as disused and spectral ruins. Such ruins as those at Gunnerside Gill are clues that the valley once supported a thriving lead-mining industry providing the lead for cathedrals and churches across the country.

From welcoming and tearoom-filled villages, such as Thwaite, Muker and Reeth to the roaring River Swale and the rolling dales themselves, this is a place that gets under your skin and leaves you yearning for more time to explore. To end as we began, with the words of James Herriot: 'I always have a feeling of loss at leaving Swaledale behind.'

St Andrew's church, reached via the Corpse Way, at Grinton.

Brontë country

❯ HAWORTH, NORTH YORKSHIRE

How to get there:

Exit M62 at Junction 24, taking
the A629 towards Keighley.
Then take the A6033 and
B6142 to Haworth.
For sat nav users: BD22 8DR
Nearest railway station:
Keighley (5 miles)
Bus services:
www.wymetro.com
0113 2457 676

The Brontë Parsonage,
from the graveyard where
the sisters now lie.

Three novels written by three sisters living in a parsonage in a small Yorkshire village were published in 1847. Writing under pseudonyms to disguise the fact they were women, Charlotte, Anne and Emily Brontë took the literary world by storm with *Jane Eyre*, *Agnes Grey* and *Wuthering Heights* after years of struggling to find a publisher. However, within eight years all three sisters had passed away, leaving the world wanting more and the village of Haworth firmly on the tourist map.

It's impossible to move in the pretty village without coming face to face with the Brontës one way or another. Visit the old apothecary at No. 84 and you'll see a plaque declaring that pharmacist Betty Hardacre used to dispense laudanum to brother Branwell Brontë from this spot. There's a sign at the school reminding you that Charlotte Brontë once taught there. There's even a stone pointing out the exact gate in the churchyard through which the Brontë sisters were carried to their final resting place.

Over the years the village has been the home to the Brontë Cinema, Brontë Guest House, Brontë Undertakers and even the Brontë Lodge of Buffaloes. As the cobbled streets are regularly pounded by the feet of their fans you can't really blame the enterprising locals.

Other things to see:

The evocative ruins of Wycoller Hall sit in the centre of the hamlet of Wycoller, 7 miles west of Haworth, and just over the border in Lancashire. The sisters often visited here and the Hall is said to be the inspiration for Ferndean Manor in *Jane Eyre*. For sat nav users: BB8

The romantic remains of Wycoller Hall, a favourite haunt of the Brontë sisters.

Brontë business has pretty much been the village's main trade since Charlotte died in 1855. Her father even had to snip Charlotte's letters into tiny fragments to send out to grieving fans as a form of relic.

Most people head straight for the Parsonage where the sisters used to write in one small room. Here the Brontë Parsonage Museum and Brontë Society set out to dispel some of the myths of this seemingly tragic, trio. Charlotte especially has repeatedly been portrayed as a neurotic, isolated woman plagued by a volatile father. But when you walk among the rooms where Charlotte, Anne and Emily lived and died you'll discover that their doom-laden personas were largely created by Charlotte herself and have been perpetuated ever since.

Since its foundation in 1893 the Brontë Society has gathered a staggeringly large collection of documents and artefacts, too many to cram into this relatively small building simultaneously. So for those who do make the pilgrimage to Haworth time and time again, there is always something new to see and learn. The lives of the Brontës are as endlessly fascinating some 150 years after their deaths as the fictional worlds they created.

Find out more:
www.bronte.org.uk
01535 642 323

John Craven **on a seaside holiday** »

As a Yorkshire boy we used to head to Whitby on holiday. My parents would rent a little cottage right at the bottom of the 199 steps that lead up to the iconic Gothic Whitby Abbey. All these years later it's still one of the best British seaside towns. It has so much to offer, from the Bram Stoker connection and Captain Cook's legacy to the Abbey itself – the location of the treaty signed in AD 664 that decided when Easter would be celebrated and paved the way for a unified England.

I remember that the bus journey from Leeds to the coast seem to drag on for ever, but as we were driving through the stunning North Yorkshire moors no one really complained.

How to get there:

Slaithwaite is located
on the A62, just north of
the Peak District.
For sat nav users: HG7 5JN
Nearest railway station:
Slaithwaite
Bus services:
www.firstgroup.com
0113 245 7676

Find out more:

www.slaithwaitemoonraking.org

Other things to see:

Just 7 miles from Slaithwaite
you'll find a small town familiar
to fans of *Last of the Summer
Wine*. For over 35 years,
Holmfirth has been the home
of Clegg and company. The
various locations used in the
world's longest-running sitcom
can be explored by foot or on a
number of bus tours.
For sat nav users: HD7 1JP
www.summerwine-holmfirth.
co.uk

'You foolish moonrakers'

▶ SLAITHWAITE, WEST YORKSHIRE

Tissue-paper lanterns
paraded at the
Slaithwaite Moonraking
Festival.

In 1802, customs men from the Yorkshire village of Slaithwaite found a group of dubious locals trying to rake up something from the canal's murky waters. Suspecting them to be smugglers attempting to recover a hidden stash of rum, the officials asked what was going on. 'Are you blind?' came the befuddled reply, 'Can't you see that the moon has fallen in the canal? We're trying to get her out before she drowns.' Sure enough, as the customs men watched, the gang of friends returned to raking hopelessly across the moon's reflection. Dismissing the men as obvious fools, the dim-witted policemen continued on their way and as soon as they were out of sight, the sniggering smugglers managed to pull the first of their barrels of contraband from their watery hiding hole.

Two centuries later, Slaithwaite (or Slaw-it, as it's pronounced by the locals) runs a bi-annual event to celebrate those wily moonrakers. Villagers fashion hundreds of tissue-paper and willow lanterns in a host of weird and wonderful designs, according to the festival's theme. As the sun sets, the lanterns are lit by candlelight and processed through the streets, accompanied by the sound of brass and jazz bands. It's a magical sight enjoyed by the 5,000 people who descend on the town, which culminates in the lanterns being floated along the canal to celebrate the original moonrakers who started it all. As fireworks burst in the skies above, the reed beds shine in the ethereal orange lights of the flickering candles.

King of the coil humpers

❯ GAWTHORPE, WEST YORKSHIRE

Coal merchant Reggie Sedgewick couldn't believe what he had just heard. Lewis Hartley had burst into the Beehive Inn in Gawthorpe, taken one look at Reggie and declared, 'Ba gum, lad, tha' looks buggered.'

'Ah'm as fit as thee, Lewis,' the outraged Sedgewick replied, 'an' if tha' dun't believe me gerra a bagga coil on thy back an 'ah'll get one on mine an 'ah'll race thee to t' top o' t' wood!'

On Easter Monday the two men lined up, hauled a bag of coil (coal to non-locals) and raced just over 1,000 metres from the Royal Oak pub to the maypole on the village green. What started as a matter of pride in 1963 (with a £10 bet on the side to make it more interesting) has now become one of Yorkshire's most popular Easter Monday customs.

Gawthorpe sits alongside one of the richest coal seams in the United Kingdom. Mining began in the 14th century but just five years after Reggie and Lewis's bet, the last mine around Gawthorpe had closed. The World Coal Carrying Championships are helping to keep alive a little of that rich industrial heritage.

In 2008, *Countryfile* sent Ben Fogle along to compete. To keep health-and-safety people happy only 30 places are made available, handed out on a first-come, first-served basis – 15 can register by post and 15 on the day. Only the previous year's winner is guaranteed a chance to compete.

Once Ben had his place secured he discovered that the rules are simple. Pick up your standard onehundredweight (or 51kg) sack of coal, swing it over your shoulders and join your fellow contestants on the starting line. The first person to drop their sack at the foot of the maypole is declared the King or Queen of the Coil Humpers.

Countryfile's action man finished in 27th place with a time of 6 minutes 10 seconds. Respectable enough, though nowhere near the world records of 4 minutes 6 seconds for the men and 5 minutes 5 seconds for the women.

How to get there:

The village of Gawthorpe is on the A638 near Ossett. For sat nav users: WF5 9AU Nearest railway station: Batley (2 miles) Bus services: www.wymetro.com 0113 245 7676

Find out more:

www.gawthorpe.ndo.co.uk 0845 601 8353

Other things to see:

Get the lowdown on Yorkshire's mining history at the National Coal Mining Museum for England in nearby Wakefield. Travel 140 metres beneath the ground to discover how conditions in mines have changed from the early 1800s to the present day. And don't worry, no coil humping is involved. For sat nav users: WF4 4RH www.ncm.org.uk 01924 848 806

The start of the men's race at the World Coal Carrying Championships.

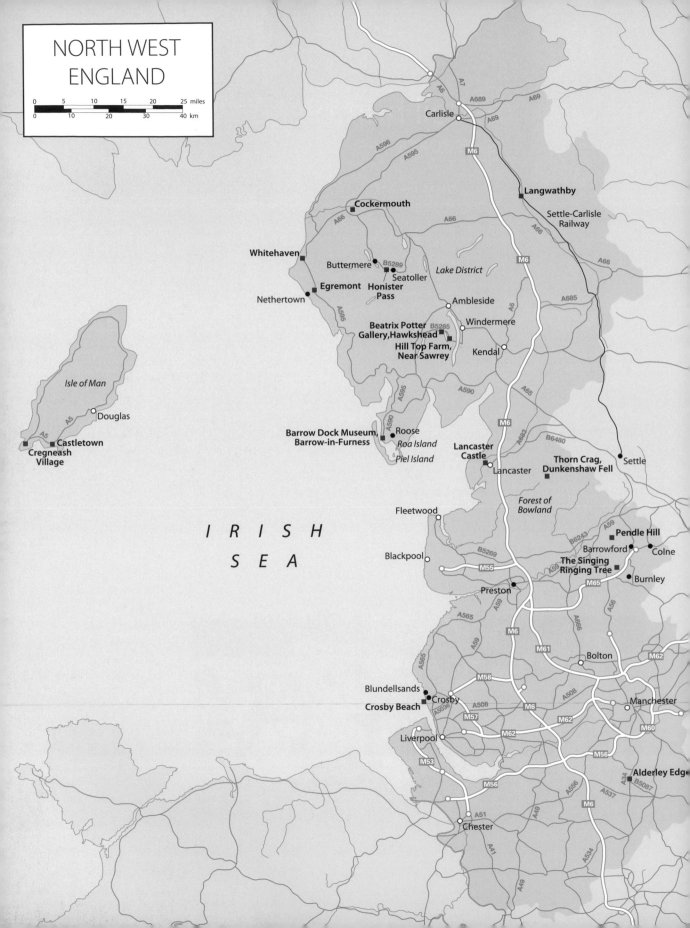

NORTH WEST ENGLAND

0 5 10 15 20 25 miles
0 10 20 30 40 km

Carlisle

A7
A6
A689
A69
A69
M6

A596
A595

Cockermouth

Langwathby

Settle-Carlisle
Railway

A66
A66
A66

Whitehaven

Buttermere
B5289
Seatoller

Lake District

M6

Egremont
Honister
Pass

Nethertown

Ambleside

Windermere

A6

A685

A595

Beatrix Potter
Gallery, Hawkshead
B5285

Hill Top Farm,
Near Sawrey

Kendal

A595

A590

A65

Isle of Man

A5
Douglas

A5
Castletown
Cregneash
Village

A590

Barrow Dock Museum,
Barrow-in-Furness

Roose
Roa Island
Piel Island

Lancaster
Castle

Lancaster

M6

A683

B6480

Thorn Crag,
Dunkenshaw Fell

Settle

*Forest of
Bowland*

Fleetwood

I R I S H

S E A

Blackpool

B5269

A59

B6243

Pendle Hill

Barrowford
Colne

The Singing
Ringing Tree

Burnley

A56

M55

Preston

A565
A59

M65

A666

A59

M6

M61

Bolton

M62

Blundellsands
Crosby

Crosby Beach

A565

M58

A508

M57

A5036

A508

M62

M6

M62

Manchester

M60

Liverpool

M53

M56

A556

M56

Alderley Edge
A34
B5087

M6

A51

Chester

A41

A49

A537

A534

North West

The Lake District is the adventure capital of Great Britain. Lovers of the great outdoors swarm here year after year to walk, ride, sail and climb. It is a landscape that has inspired great works of literature from Wordsworth to Beatrix Potter, and encouraged people to risk their lives to mine its riches. There's good humour in those hills too. Here a simple pub landlord can be a king and the world's ugliest face find glory.

But what of the rest of the region? What of the wizards and witches of Lancashire and Cheshire, the last stronghold of Britain's most endangered bird of prey and one of the best railway journeys on the planet? In the North West, industry blossomed, failed and then fought back, finding new ways to keep the spirit of the past alive, while across the water the inhabitants of the Isle of Man doggedly kept their independence (if you go to the World Tin Bath Championships in Castletown never make the mistake of calling England the mainland!). This is a place where people have faced challenge and hardship and won through, feats just as impressive as those Lakeland peaks.

Your face will stay like that

❯ EGREMONT CRAB FAIR, CUMBRIA

How to get there:

Egremont is found on the A595.

For sat nav users: CA22 2DW

Nearest railway station:

Nethertown (3 miles)

Bus services:

www.stagecoachbus.com

01452 418 630

The Forest of Bowland

(previous page).

The Crab Fair at Egremont was first held in 1267 after Henry II granted Thomas de Multon, the lord of the manor, a royal charter to hold a weekly market and an annual apple fair. Every harvest, the serfs of the region headed to the manor house laden with crab apples, vegetables and corn to pay their dues.

In celebration, de Multon threw a series of games in the hope that such frivolity would help his people forget the poverty and hardship of the previous year. Some of the activities, such as bull-baiting and cock-fighting, have long been outlawed, but the majority of the downright silly contests have survived. One of the favourites is the greasy-pole challenge: contestants have to scramble up a 9-metre pole to grab either the ribbons positioned strategically up the pole or the side of mutton that is nailed to the top. Oh, and to make it a little more difficult, the pole is slathered with lard.

If that seems a little on the dangerous side, you could try your hand at the pipe-smoking competitions, horn-blowing, fancy-dress wheelbarrow races or Cumberland wrestling. One of the least strenuous pastimes is trying to catch the apples that are thrown from the back of a wagon into the crowd. In days gone by these would have been the crab apples that gave the festival its name. If you've ever bitten into a crab apple, you will know the effect it can have – many a serf must have pulled a series of funny faces as the bitter flavour of the apple hit home.

Which brings us on to the fair's finale – the infamous World Gurning Championships. It's a very simple game. You come on to a stage, stick your head into a horse brace (or 'braffin') and pull the most hideous face you can manage for 60 seconds. No props are allowed and glasses must be removed. You are judged on how disgusting your expression is as well as how different your contorted face is to your usual countenance.

In a particularly cruel moment, *Countryfile* sent Michaela Strachan to compete in the women's version of the championship in 2002. Amazingly, she walked away with the first prize!

The World Champion Gurner 2008 (above); Egremont crab apples ready for harvesting (opposite page).

Other things to see:
Egremont Castle, its sandstone ruins visible above the town's main street, was the target of Scottish raids almost as soon as it was constructed in around 1120 by William de Meschines. By the end of the 16th century the castle had deteriorated, helped along by the locals who had taken the sandstone for their own houses, leaving the gatehouse, part of the great hall and a curtain wall.

Find out more:
www.egremontcrabfair.com
07092 031 363

John Craven discovers Cockermouth »

When people visit the Lake District they head for the honeypots like Bowness on Windermere and Hawkshead and miss out on gems like Cockermouth. This beautiful Georgian town on the northernmost edge of the Lake District National Park is located between two hills, at the confluence of the rivers Cocker and Derwent. Cockermouth is steeped in history. Mary Queen of Scots fled here after her defeat at the battle of Langside but the town's most famous resident was William Wordsworth, who was born here in 1770 and grew up in Wordsworth House, now maintained by the National Trust.

Cockermouth hit the headlines due to the dreadful floods of late 2009, but perhaps some good will come out of that particular tragedy as people realise what a wonderful place it is to visit.

The tale of Beatrix Potter

> ❯ HILL TOP FARM, CUMBRIA

How to get there:

Hill Top Farm is found in
the village of Near Sawrey, on
the B5285 from Ambleside.
The house is open to the
public 14 Feb–1 Nov.
For sat nav users: LA22 0LF
Nearest railway station:
Windermere (4½ miles)
Bus services:
www.mountain-goat.com
01539 445 161

Find out more:

www.nationaltrust.org.uk/
hilltop
01539 436 269

Other things to see:

The Beatrix Potter Gallery in
Hawkshead is based in the
offices of Beatrix Potter's
solicitor and husband, William
Heelis. Many of her original
paintings are on display.
For sat nav users: LA22 0NS
www.nationaltrust.org.uk/
beatrixpotter
01539 436 355

If you know where to look, walking through the Lake District is literally like stepping into a children's book, specifically the tales of Beatrix Potter. To most people, the island in the middle of Derwent Water is St Herberts but for fans of Squirrel Nutkin, it is Owl Island. Just to the west of Derwent Water, you'll find Newlands Valley, home to Mrs Tiggy-Winkle while Jeremy Fisher was often seen punting over Esthwaite Water.

Beatrix Potter had been introduced to the Lake District while holidaying as a child but it wasn't until 1905 that she owned her own patch of Lakeland. Using the royalties from her books she bought Hill Top Farm, which would become the setting of the tales of Samuel Whiskers and Tom Kitten. It also became central to the next phase of her life.

Over the years, Beatrix Potter had developed a close friendship with Hardwicke Rawnsley, the Canon of Wray. Rawnsley – who went on to become one of the founders of the National Trust – was concerned that the age of rapid development in which they lived was a threat to the Lake District. Beatrix Potter shared his views and started to buy property around Hill Top at first to extend her estate but later to prevent it being bought up by railway companies and developers.

Beatrix Potter visited Hill Top as often as she could, using it as a writing studio and a place to entertain guests, but it wasn't until 1913 that she finally made the move to the Lake District. From this point on, her writing career began to slow as she devoted herself to farming. Beatrix Potter was soon seen out on her tenanted farms, rolling up her sleeves and getting stuck in, searching for lost animals and wading through mud to unblock drains. She became an enthusiastic breeder and judge of the hardy but endangered Herdwick sheep and was due to become president of the Herdwick Breeders Association shortly before her death in 1943. Her very last letter was to one of her shepherds and her entire estate – 1,600 hectares (4,000 acres) of land, 14 farms, her Herdwick sheep and scores of houses – was left to the Rawnsley National Trust.

Following Beatrix Potter's death, her husband William Heelis scattered her ashes at Hill Top. While no one knows the exact location, Beatrix Potter's true legacy lives on in the Cumbrian landscape she did so much to preserve.

Hill Top Farm in
Near Sawrey near
Esthwaite Water.

All hail the king

> ❯ PIEL ISLAND, CUMBRIA

How to get there:

In summer, you can get to
Piel by ferry from Roa Island
or, if you're feeling more
adventurous (and have checked
the tide times carefully), you
can walk across the sands
at low tides.
For sat nav users: LA13 0QN
(Roa Island)
Nearest railway station:
Roose (4 miles)
There is no bus service.

Find out more:

www.golakes.co.uk
01229 876 505

Other things to see:

The King of Piel's throne and
crown are kept in the Barrow
Dock Museum in Barrow-in-
Furness. Built over a graving or
dry dock, the museum tracks
the development of Barrow
from a 19th-century hamlet to
a major shipbuilding centre.
Admission is free.
For sat nav users: LA14 2PW
www.dockmuseum.org.uk
01229 876 400

If you think that Queen Elizabeth II is the only reigning monarch in the United Kingdom
think again. If you were to land on the 8-hectare (20-acre) island of Piel, nearly four miles
off the coast near Barrow-in-Furness you would find yourself under the rule of a very
different sovereign.

In 1487, a merchant's son by the name of Lambert Simnel travelled to Piel from Ireland
in an attempt to dethrone Henry VII. Setting foot on this tiny scrap of English soil, he claimed
he was the Earl of Warwick and therefore the rightful King. He didn't get far. His army was
defeated by Henry's men at Stoke-on-Trent but the legacy of the king of Piel endured. These
days the title is granted to the landlord of the Ship Inn, which was built in 1836, rather than
a pretender to the English throne.

The duties of this king aren't exactly statesmanlike. He is charged with serving pints and
keeping the island tidy, but he can bestow a very special knighthood. To become a knight
of Piel you have to display certain characteristics. First of all, you need to be a man of fine
character, although that should never outweigh the other requirements of the role. A good
knight is a passionate lover of women, should enjoy a cigarette or two and is quick to buy a
round. There are of course a few perks. If for any reason you find yourself shipwrecked off Piel,
you can demand lodgings, food and drink and also have the pick of any women on the island.
Not that there are many to choose from.
The King of Piel and his family are the
only inhabitants of the island, which is
also home to a small, but impressive,
castle. This ruin has nothing to do with
the pretender kings as it was built to
protect the monks of Furness Abbey
from Scottish raids and later became
a stronghold for smugglers. Today, it's
the wildlife of Piel that is protected and
the island has been designated a Site of
Special Scientific Interest, largely for its
shingle beaches.

A new king of Piel gets a soaking
in beer at his coronation (right);
Piel Island with its ruined 14th-
century castle (opposite).

Matt Baker scrambles down the Lake District ❯❯

I was first introduced to the Lake District on an adventure trip in my third year at comprehensive school. Countless childhood holidays to the Lakes followed so I was really pleased that Julia and I marked our first episode of *Countryfile* with a jaunt back to Lakeland. What better place to find our feet than the magical Lakes?

In fact, finding my feet was one of the challenges I faced when Ghyll Scrambling. This involves basically trying to find the best route down Cumbrian mountain streams. You slide down on your bum, leap into plunge pools or put your body through all kinds of contortions in order to squeeze through narrow gaps. With a qualified instructor to guide us, our group literally threw themselves into the adventure, following the natural flow of the water through some stunning landscape.

The gateway to the Lakes
❯ WHITEHAVEN, CUMBRIA

How to get there:
Exit the M6 at Junction 40 and
follow the signs on the A66 and
A595 to Whitehaven.
For sat nav users: CA28 7JG
Nearest railway station:
Whitehaven
Bus services:
www.stagecoachbus.com/
cumbria
01228 597 222

Find out more:
www.visitcumbria.com
01946 598 914

Other things to see:
Discover the dark spirit of
Whitehaven with a small but
perfectly formed attraction.
The Rum Story is housed
within the 18th-century
shop and warehouses of the
Jefferson family. The superb
kinetic clock in the courtyard
helps explain how sugar
grown under a Caribbean
sun became the liquor that
helped build Whitehaven's
fortunes, while vivid displays
reveal the shocking truth of the
accompanying slave trade.
For sat nav users: CA28 7DN
www.therumstory.co.uk
01946 592 933

'I remember being struck,' wrote William Wordsworth in 1852, 'by the town and port of
Whitehaven, and the white waves breaking against its quays and piers.' The poet goes on
to remark that his sister was so impressed by the scene before them that she immediately
burst into tears.

In the 1990s many people shed a tear for what had become of Whitehaven. Before the
17th century the fishing village of Whitehaven was a quiet and unassuming place, but that
all changed when the Lowther family started to mine for coal around 1630. Success in one
heavy industry meant that others soon followed and Whitehaven became the first new
planned town since the Renaissance. Built on a grid system that is said to have inspired
the designers of New York, Whitehaven boomed. By the 18th century it was the second-
largest port after London and soon tobacco, rum and slaves were flooding in from the
New World, while the entire city of Dublin was supplied with coal from the Whitehaven area.

The industrial heart of Whitehaven continued to pump strongly well into the 20th century and by the 1990s the port was still a significant importer, albeit of a different commodity: phosphates for the chemical industry.

The last deep mine in the North West closed in 1986 and seven years later imports of phosphates ceased, a precursor of the wholesale exodus of the chemical industries from the region at the turn of the 21st century. Whitehaven soon began to deteriorate, the tidal port abandoned. But the people weren't about to let their town go. This was a place steeped in history, with more listed buildings than Bath and coastline that could give Cornwall a run for its money. So where heavy industry moved out, tourism moved in.

Today the Georgian town deserves to be better known than it is. Its streets are lined with grand and colourful 18th-century houses, the historic harbour has been transformed by a buzzing marina that hosts a maritime festival every other year and the town's fishing fleet has been saved. When the skies cloud over there are plenty of attractions to turn to – including the newly refurbished Beacon Museum where you can find out how Whitehaven fought off America's only attempted invasion of Britain in 1778 – but when the sun shines and you walk out just 10 minutes from the town centre you too can experience the wonder that moved Dorothy Wordsworth to tears 150 years ago.

The busy harbour at Whitehaven; Beacon Museum is on the right.

The iron road

❯ HONISTER PASS, BORROWDALE, CUMBRIA

How to get there:

Honister Pass is on the B5289
between Buttermere and
Seatoller. The mine is signposted.
For sat nav users: CA12 5XN
Nearest railway station:
Windermere (29 miles)
Bus services:
www.dokeswick.com
0870 608 2608

Find out more:
www.honister-slate-mine.co.uk
01768 777 714

The via ferrata – or iron road – craze begin in Italy during the First World War. To guide troops safely over the Dolomites a permanent cable was fastened to the mountain sides and soldiers clipped themselves to this lifeline to make sure they didn't fall. Rope bridges were thrown over more difficult locations and ladders were installed at various sections of the route.

When peace resumed, iron roads became a popular way of introducing less experienced adventure seekers to the adrenalin rush of rock climbing. Via-ferrata courses started popping up all around the world, but amazingly it wasn't until 2007 that one was installed in Britain's mountain scenery.

Slate has been mined at Honister since Roman times, although it wasn't quarried on a significant scale until 1750. By 1833 underground mines had opened to complement the overground quarries. In 1986, after almost three centuries of mining slate, Honister was facing closure, and a loss of jobs and traditional skills. But unlike the fate of many other mines, that wasn't the end of Honister. Eleven years later, chance lent a hand when Borrowdale businessman Mark Weir was taking his grandfather on a helicopter flight across the area.

Workings of the Honister Slate Mine on Great Crag, Honister Pass (opposite); the via ferrata starts with an intimidating but perfectly safe 'bridge' crossing made of railway tracks embedded across a steep gully (left).

When they passed over the slate works, the old man, who had been a Honister miner in his youth, couldn't believe the mine had closed. Moved by his grandfather's reaction, Weir and Bill Taylor, the son of another miner, bought the mine and reopened it in 2007 as a heritage enterprise – primarily as a tourist attraction but also to ensure that quality slate would once again be mined here. But it was Mark Weir's brainwave to use the Victorian miners' precipitous route to work as the location for Britain's first via ferrata that has put Honister on the modern tourist map.

The Honister via ferrata follows the Victorian miners' climb, thousands of feet above the ground. Beginning a shift at 8 am, the miners would cling to the crag as they ascended 650 metres to Fleetwick Pike in all weathers, ready for a hard day's slog. Amazingly, after loading a sledge with over 220kg of slate, they would descend the same treacherous route, pulling the sledge behind them.

Thankfully, the via ferrata means that you can make the same ascent in complete safety, attached to the fixed cable by means of lanyards and clips. The climb can be attempted by fit individuals over the age of 10 and in the main it isn't that tricky if you have a head for heights. Of course, when you're this high up, there have to be a few thrills, such as the Titanic Exposure. This section of the iron road allows you to walk to a cliff face, clip yourself on and hang over the edge. If that weren't enough excitement, a zip wire has recently been added to push the fear factor to the limit!

Other things to see:

If you don't fancy tackling the via ferrata, there are three underground tours of Honister slate mines available: Kimberly, for all ages, the Edge, for more experienced hill walkers and the Cathedral, a bespoke tour of the mine by Mark Weir himself. You can even take home some of the slate yourself. You'd be in good company: Honister green slate has roofed London's Ritz, St Paul's Cathedral and even Buckingham Palace.

Witch way to go

❯ PENDLE HILL, LANCASHIRE

How to get there:

Start by visiting the Pendle
Heritage Centre in Barrowford,
signposted a mile from
Junction 13 of the M65.
For sat nav users: BB9 6JQ
Nearest railway station:
Colne (2 miles)
Bus services:
www.tyrertours.com
01282 611 123

Find out more:

www.htnw.co.uk
01282 677 150

Other things to see:

Lancaster Castle, where the
witches finally met their end,
is still a working prison and
court with two sittings per
day, although guided tours are
available all year round, except
for Christmas and New Year.
For sat nav users: LA1 1YJ
www.lancastercastle.com
01524 64998

The panoramic view
from Pendle Hill.

If you believe the movies, you couldn't move in 16th- and 17th-century England without tripping over a practitioner of black magic. The truth, as always, is slightly less interesting but one particular case has gone down in history, its name for ever linked to dark forces and unnatural acts: the Pendle Witch Trial.

In the ninth year of James I's reign, two families lived in the shadow of the mighty Pendle Hill: the Chattoxes and the Demdikes. Both families were ruled by old matriarchs who hated each other with a passion. They were believed by the locals to be witches, a reputation neither woman tried to disprove as it worked in their favour, allowing them to gain work as healers or to extort money.

In the end it would be their undoing. In March 1612, one of the Demdike clan, Alizon Device, was arrested under suspicion of witchcraft and immediately confessed, implicating her grandmother and the Chattoxes to boot. This kick-started a series of events that would have 19 people thrown into the dungeons beneath Lancaster Castle, where they were kept for five months on a diet of gruel and bread. Ten went to the gallows, while old Mother Demdike died in jail.

The macabre tale has attracted tourists ever since. To wet your wiccan whistle there's even a 45-mile car trail that starts and ends at the Pendle Heritage Centre in Barrowford, which is packed with information about witches.

In all the locations that feature in the grisly account – picturesque villages such as Barley, Downham and Rimington – one player dominates every scene. At 557 metres Pendle Hill towers over the area; had it been another 20 metres, Pendle would be officially classified as a mountain. From its summit on a clear day you can make out the three peaks of Yorkshire, with the Pennines to your east, and even the odd glimpse of the Isle of Man to the west. It was here in 1652 that George Fox, after a troublesome climb to the peak, believed he received a vision from the Lord to gather a great group of people. On his return to the foot of the hill he founded the Quaker movement, almost as an antidote to the devilish tales of women practising the dark arts on the long ridge of Pendle.

Julia Bradbury searches for the Pendle witches »

The one thing you can never be sure about on *Countryfile* is the weather, but it couldn't have been more appropriate when we visited the Forest of Bowland to track down the infamous Pendle witches. We were there for Hallowe'en and it was certainly spooky. As soon as I stepped out of the car I knew we were in for a bitterly, bitterly cold day and, true enough, the winds were whipping up a storm.

It's a place that I'm going to have to return to soon, because Pendle Hill itself is beautiful in fine weather, but on this particular shoot I was constantly squinting against the wind. The atmosphere suited the story though. I could almost hear someone whisper 'When shall we three meet again?' on the wind.

John Craven on his favourite Yorkshire dale »

Wharfedale was where it all started for me. My first real taste of the countryside came when I jumped on my bike from my home on the outskirts of Leeds and rode to Wharfedale. As I got older, the bikes got bigger and we would head up to the top of Buckden Pike, towering over the valley. In my late teens I used to do quite a bit of caving with a group of pals, exploring Dow Cave in Kettlewell – a great adventure for young lads.

I still go back as much as possible. Wharfedale is the most beautiful of the seven dales. The southern area is quite built up around the towns of Ilkley and Otley, birthplace of Thomas Chippendale, the famous cabinetmaker. But head further north and you're in a land of stunning hill meadows and little windy lanes that has hardly changed since my childhood.

The brink of extinction
❯ FOREST OF BOWLAND, LANCASHIRE

An hour's drive from the conurbations where 11 million people live is one of the north west's hidden treasures, the Forest of Bowland, 300 square miles of remote, heather-covered peat-bog moorland. Not a forest in the traditional sense, Bowland was a hunting ground for Norman kings, taking its name from 'Boland' meaning the land of cattle. The dome-topped hills, so easily missed if your only experience of the Lancashire landscape is roaring past on the M6, stand over unpretentious villages, beautiful woods and sparkling streams. Is it any wonder that the Queen has said that, if she could retire, she would make Bowland her home?

The area is dominated by some of Britain's best red-grouse moors, heavily managed despite their appearance of a sweeping wilderness and emaciated gritstone tors. The high numbers of red grouse on the plains mean that the Forest of Bowland has become a hotspot for Britain's most threatened bird of prey: the hen harrier. Since 1999 a project has been run by Natural England, Lancashire Constabulary, the RSPB and the shooting tenants and gamekeepers of the local United Utilities estate to protect the birds, and their numbers speak for themselves. Unlike in other areas of the country, the gamekeepers who manage the shooting estates tolerate the birds, accepting their part in the local environment, meaning that around 50 per cent of England's breeding population of hen harriers now nest in Bowland. That figure is put into stark relief when you realise that it only amounts to between six and ten pairs.

While the hen harrier hovers over the brink of extinction in England, the work in the Forest of Bowland gives a glimmer of hope and means this is the best place for birdwatchers to catch an all-too-rare glimpse of the awe-inspiring bird. The male hen harrier is easier to spot: a pale-grey bird, almost like a seagull, distinct against the green of the landscape. The female is more cryptically coloured with brown wings and a white rump, which is easier to see as the day wanes.

How to get there:
A good starting point is the Bowland Visitor Centre in Beacon Fell Country Park. Leave the M55 at Junction 1, taking the A6 north and then the B5269, following the signs to Beacon Fell.
For sat nav users: PR3 2NL
Nearest railway station: Preston (11 miles)
Bus services:
www.stagecoachbus.com
01524 422 217

Find out more:
www.forestofbowland.com
01995 640 557

Other things to see:
Standing in glorious isolation but just 20 minutes from the M6, Thorn Crag sits on the slopes of Dunkenshaw Fell. Notoriously difficult to climb, the gritstone crag is said to have been another inspiration for J. R. R. Tolkien's Middle Earth.

The green valleys and heather-covered fens of Little Crag above Little Dale in the Forest of Bowland (opposite); a hen harrier with chicks (left).

The wizard and the white horse

❯ ALDERLEY EDGE, CHESHIRE

How to get there:

The Edge is 1½ miles from
Alderley village on the B5087
and is signposted.
For sat nav users: SK9
Nearest railway station:
Alderley Edge (1½ miles)
Bus services:
www.traveline-northwest.co.uk
0871 200 22 33

Other things to see:

In the 21st century, the nearby
village of Alderley Edge is one
third of the so-called 'golden
triangle' along with Presbury
and Wilmslow, a mecca for
the rich and ostentatious and
positively crawling with premier
footballers. The arrival of the
likes of Wayne Rooney and Ole
Gunnar Solskjaer have caused
controversy as the footballers
have been bulldozing 1930s
cottages to make way for
ultra-modern mansions.
So you might get to see some
more familiar faces out on
the Edge. Whatever would
Merlin have thought?

The enigmatic sandstone escarpment known as the Edge
rises 150 metres above the Cheshire Plain, covered by thick
oak and beech woodland and riddled with hidden entrances
to Bronze Age mines. In the middle of the wood, just below
Castle Rock, where Mesolithic hunter–gatherers would have
gazed across to the Pennines, you'll find a little wishing well,
guarded over by a moss-covered face carved into the very stone.
Beneath its eerie aspect, a well-worn inscription invites you to
'Drink of this and take thy fill, for the water falls by the wizhard's
[sic] will.' The sorcerer in question is said to be none other than
Merlin himself.

The legend of Alderley Edge tells of a farmer who was on
his way to the market at Macclesfield to sell his prize white mare.
A bedraggled old man stopped him at the large ditch in the
wood known today as Thieves' Hole, offering to buy the horse
for a modest price. Insulted, the farmer continued but although
his horse attracted praise at market no one would offer a penny
for it. Dejected, the farmer returned through the wood, only to
meet the bearded man once again. He was led by the old soul
to a stone that split in two with the sound of rolling thunder to
expose an ancient chamber. The old man revealed that he was
Merlin, and explained that King Arthur and his army lay asleep
beneath the woodland, ready to spring into action if needed by
England's crown. The problem was, they were one white steed
short. Terrified that he had refused the legendary magician, the
farmer gladly took his purse of coins and fled the chamber. The
gates of rock crashed closed behind him and Merlin, the horse
and Arthur's resting place were never seen again.

Local author Alan Garner claims his stonemason grandfather
carved the inscription above the wizard's well and also
constructed the Druids' circle of stones that lies between Stormy
Point and the Beacon at the highest point of the Edge. Be
that as it may, the legend of Merlin and the white mare were
the inspiration for Garner's fantasy novels *The Weirdstone of
Brisingamen* (1960) and *The Moon of Gomrath* (1963).

The Druids' circle of
stones in autumn,
Alderley Edge.

Waiting for the sun

▶ CROSBY BEACH, MERSEYSIDE

On a quiet beach, just eight miles from Liverpool, 100 men stand gazing out to sea. Unmoving and silent, they don't flinch as a chilly sea laps around their ankles, gradually creeping up to their chests. As the ocean presses against them, there is no struggle or panic. Their vigil over the waves is unending, day in, day out.

Your first sight of the lone figures is often an unsettling one. Then as you approach you realise that these sentinels aren't flesh and blood, but cold, hard cast-iron, each weighing 650 kilos. This is 'Another Place', a permanent installation on the Sefton coast by artist Antony Gormley, best known for Gateshead's 'Angel of the North' or the 'Fourth Plinth' in Trafalgar Square.

Dotted over almost two miles of Crosby Beach, with some standing out in the sea, the 100 figures are cast from a mould of Gormley's own body. Over time they will be worn by the weather, giving each a unique and timeless texture. Serene and peaceful, the sculptures stare out to sea, all facing the same direction as if they were joined in a kind of ancient ritual.

The installation first came to Crosby in 2005 having been displayed in Germany, Norway and Belgium. The silent watchers were only intended to stand guard for 18 months before being shipped off to New York in 2007 but after a change of heart from both Gormley and Sefton Council, the artwork is now a permanent fixture. There were some detractors, including conservationists, worried that increased visitor numbers would affect wildlife, and coastguards who claimed that the submerged statues would be a danger to boats. Gormley dismissed the concerns as part of Britain's increasingly risk-averse culture and insisted that Crosby was the perfect place for his metal men. Certainly no one other than the sculptures themselves should try to take a dip in the waters along the beach because there is an extremely dangerous rip-tide.

So Gormley's iron legion remains, a work of art that changes every second, depending on the light, the tide and your own reaction.

Other things to see:
More public art is found in the Panopticon installations around Lancashire, a series of sculptures, each set on a high point overlooking spectacular scenery. The Singing Ringing Tree at Crown Point above the town of Burnley is a twisted sculpture of pipes and steel. Other Panopticons are located at Blackburn, Haslingden and Wycoller Park.
www.visitlancashire.com
01282 421 986

How to get there:
Take the M57 or M58 to Switch Island and then follow the A5036 until you pick up signs to Crosby and Antony Gormley's 'Another Place'.
Nearest railway station: Blundellsands & Crosby (1 mile)
Bus services:
www.merseytravel.gov.uk
0870 608 2608

Find out more:
www.visitliverpool.com
0151 233 2008

One of the sculptures from Antony Gormley's installation 'Another Place' (opposite); Crosby Beach at sunset (overleaf).

That sinking feeling

❯ WORLD TIN BATH CHAMPIONSHIPS, ISLE OF MAN

How to get there:

Castletown can be found off
the A3 or A5.

For sat nav users: IM9

Nearest railway station:

Castletown

Bus services:

www.iombusandrail.info

01624 662 525

Airports: Ronaldsway connects
the Isle of Man with all the main
UK airports.

Ferries: www.steam-packet.com

08722 992 992

Find out more:

www.visitisleofman.com

01624 627 443

Other things to see:

Castletown is dominated by
its 13th-century Castle
Rushen, one of the most finely
preserved medieval castles
in Europe. Many rooms in the
fortress have been decorated
to represent different eras in
its long history.

For sat nav users: IM9 1LF

www.storyofmann.com

01624 648 000

In 2006, Ben Fogle rowed across the Atlantic in 49 days, 19 hours and 8 minutes. After such a herculean task, surely *Countryfile*'s action man could cope with paddling a tin bath across a harbour in the Isle of Man?

The World Tin Bath Championships have been running since 1971 in Castletown, the ancient capital of Man. It all started when the Castletown Ale Drinkers Society was asked to put on a fundraising event at the town carnival. Knowing that people love to see other folk plunge into water, the drinking club organised a man-powered flight competition. To add a bit of originality seven guys in seven tin baths were on hand to paddle across to the crashed fliers and pull them out of the harbour. When every magnificent man in their flying machine had ended up head first in the drink, the society realised that they still had some time to kill. 'Race you to the end of the harbour!' came the cry and the other six tin-bathers took up the challenge. The race was so popular that by the following year it had become an event in its own right.

The Drinkers Society gave it a shelf life of ten years but thought it was a fun way to raise money for local Isle of Man charities. Four decades on, the race is still being held and two of those original seven from 1971 still dust off their baths every year: Holmes Blackburn – who has converted his bath to resemble a Viking longboat – and David Collister, the race organiser. There are a few rules. Your bath must be single-hulled, made of metal and should not exceed 1.5 metres in length. For obvious reasons it needs to be fitted with a buoyancy aid although the organisers admit that they expect to see around 50 per cent sinking. After all, who wants to see everyone kept dry?

Which brings us back to Ben. On that warm August afternoon back in 2007, Ben stepped into the specially designed *Countryfile* tub … and sank. Three times. Before even leaving the jetty. Eventually, armed with a new and bigger bath, Ben was off and successfully rowed the 182 metres, only to sink on the finishing line. There was just one snag. The man who had rowed from America to England managed to get hypothermia after the World Tin Bath Championships in the Irish Sea.

But the organisers were impressed: 'Ben was brilliant to be honest,' admits David Collister. 'He was one of the very first guys I've seen sink, climb up a vertical ladder, refloat his bath and get back in. There've only been two people in 39 years who have actually done that.'

Competitors battle it out
at the World Tin Bath
Championships.

Matt Baker on the Isle of Man »

I was really taken with the Isle of Man. You can see why so many film units visit the island to replicate various parts of the UK. Here you'll find landscapes from mountain to moorland – all within a few miles of each other. One minute we were filming on a lovely beach and the next we turned a corner and could have been on the west coast of Scotland.

Take Cregneash village, for example, where I delivered turnips from the back of a horse and cart. One of the oldest villages on Man, Cregneash was untouched by modern technology until the 1900s. Today it's largely a living museum, giving you a glimpse of what Manx life was like in years gone by. However, it also doubled as Tullymore in the film *Waking Ned*, when the producers couldn't find an Irish village that they thought looked Irish enough, and has even doubled as a Scottish highland community in a Lassie movie.

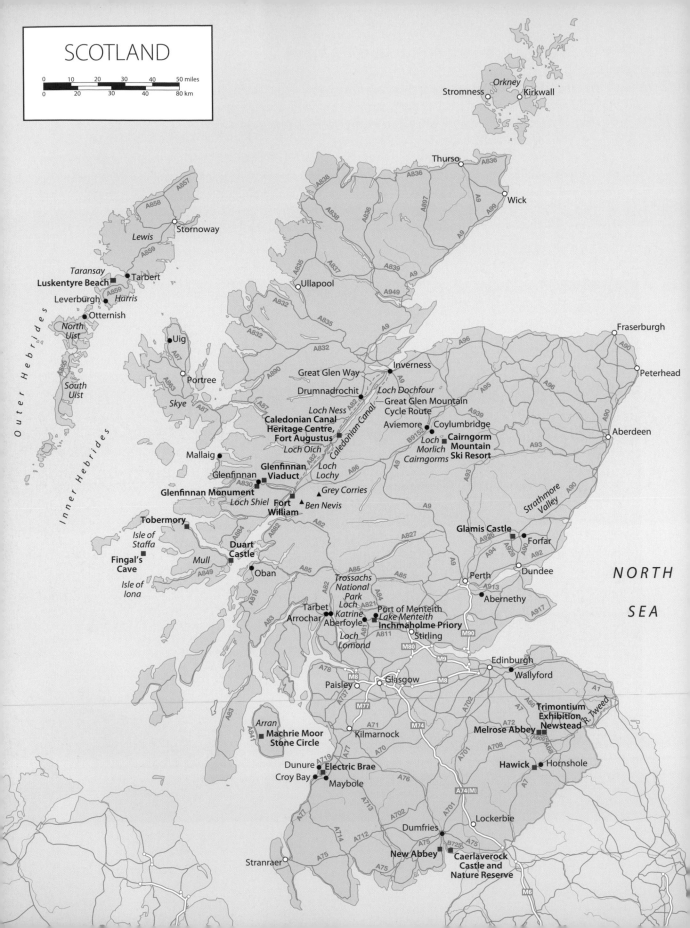

Scotland

Scotland has long been a country fraught with conflict.
The English border was a dangerous place to live as
raiding parties often crossed over to rampage and
pillage. Some of these blood-thirsty encounters are
remembered through such customs as the Common
Ridings or given a permanent memorial in ruined
fortresses like Caerlaverock Castle or the monument
to the unknown Highlander at Glenfinnan.

Scotland today fights hard to maintain its cultural
heritage and remarkable wildlife. Sea eagles swoop over
the Isle of Mull as near by the artisans of Harris still weave
the nation's finest tweed. Loch Lomond and the Trossachs
National Park is a perfect example of how modern
leisure pursuits such as speed-boating can co-exist with
conservation, while the Great Trossachs Forest project aims
to establish a future woodland the size of Glasgow.

Whether or not the heart of Robert the Bruce is really
buried at Melrose Abbey, the enduring spirit of Britain's last
great wilderness will soon carve a special place in yours.

The island that sings
❯ ISLE OF STAFFA, INNER HEBRIDES

How to get there:
Boats trips run regularly from the isle of Iona and from Oban on the mainland but only some boats from Mull land on Staffa. For sat nav users: PA65 6AY There are no train or bus services.

Find out more:
www.nts.org.uk
0844 493 2237

Other things to see:
Nearby Mull is the largest of Argyll & Bute's Atlantic islands and has one of the highest concentrations of golden eagles in Europe. Also look out for sea eagles, distinguishable by their white tails, reintroduced to Mull in the 1970s.

Highland cattle in the Trossachs National Park (previous page); the basalt-columned entrance to Fingal's cave (opposite).

In 1829 German-born Felix Mendelssohn was touring Scotland. On 7 August he boarded a paddle steamer set to pass the Staffa or Pillar Island, a small, uninhabited isle 6 miles west of Mull that boasts a unique beauty. Its cliff line is almost entirely made up of giant hexagonal basalt columns, the northern end of the Giant's Causeway that starts in Antrim, Northern Ireland (see page 218). Formed around 60 million years ago, when molten lava came in contact with water and rapidly cooled, the columns are so regular you have to keep reminding yourself that you're looking at a natural phenomenon.

Staffa has numerous small caves but none so evocative as Fingal's Cave. Barely 12 metres across at its widest point, it is lined with the same rock pillars, which stretch up to the ceiling like the pipes of a gigantic organ.

Mendelssohn's journey was not a smooth one and the composer was violently seasick. Yet even as his stomach lurched with the horizon, the mesmerising sound of the waves crashing against the basalt columns had a profound effect. Immediately inspired, he scribbled down 20 bars of music, which he later rushed off to his sister in a letter. Those few bars would form the opening of his 1830 *Hebrides Overture*. The completed work, also known as *Fingal's Cave*, mirrors the remote stateliness of the Scottish coast and immortalised the little Hebridean island.

Fingal's Cave is one of the world's most famous caverns and yet hardly anyone ever visits it. Certainly, the majority of those who gaze open-mouthed at the natural wonder do so from the safety of a passing pleasure craft, but it is possible to visit. A few boats will land on Staffa to give you an hour or so to wander near where razorbills, guillemots and puffins nest. An uneven pathway takes you down to the cave mouth, and once inside some of the shorter pillars act as stepping stones.

It is fitting to note, as you pull away from the hauntingly beautiful island, that the Gaelic name for Fingal's Cave, *Uamh Binne*, translates appropriately enough as 'the cave where the sea makes music'.

John Craven on the Isle of Mull ❯❯

The wonderful self-contained microcosm of Scotland has everything. I love visiting Tobermory, a beautiful little fishing town with charming different-coloured houses. This is where the BBC children's series *Balamory* was based. You can get absolutely gorgeous scallops and chips for next to nothing from a mobile fish and chips on the quay here.

Then there's wonderful Duart Castle, the ancestral home of the Clan Maclean since the 13th century. The view from the ramparts of Duart, looking out over the Sound of Mull, is one of the best I know.

A Hebridean odyssey

> ❯ ISLE OF HARRIS, OUTER HEBRIDES

Have you ever wanted to walk on the moon? Well, the east coast of Harris may be as near as you can get in the British Isles. Harris is joined to its twin Lewis in the north west of the Outer Hebrides (also known as the Western Isles). It's an island of two halves. The east is rugged, almost lunar in landscape, and for good reason. The rough, grey rock is known in geological circles as anorthosite and shares the characteristics of similar rocks brought back from the moon. Science-fiction fans may even have watched *Na Baigh* (the bays) of Harris repeatedly without realising it. In the 1960s Stanley Kubrick filmed the island from the air, using special tinted lenses, to represent the planet Jupiter in his epic film *2001: A Space Odyssey*.

At 798 metres An Cliseam is the highest mountain both on Harris and in the entire Outer Hebrides. With winds that whip in from the Atlantic at 100mph, this is terrain best left to experienced walkers and climbers.

Everything changes on the west coast as harsh mountains give way to fertile *machair* (plains of coastal grassland) and white, sandy beaches. The best has to be Luskentyre, a stretch of stunning sandy beach fringed by vast sand-dunes to the north. Behind you the North Harris mountains loom on the horizon while the beautiful island of Taransay, home to the BBC's *Castaway 2000*, where we first met Ben Fogle, can be seen over the turquoise sea. It's fair to say that if you could transport Luskentyre to warmer climes it would become one of the most popular beaches in the world. As it is, there's every chance you may have this dazzling white paradise all to yourself.

How to get there:
Car ferries run between Tarbert on Harris and Uig on Skye, while you can also get to Leverburgh from Otternish on North Uist. For sat nav users: HD3 3DJ
Car ferries: www.calmac.co.uk
0800 066 5000
Bus services:
www.leverburgh.co.uk
01859 502 441

Find out more:
www.explore-harris.com
08452 255 121

Other things to see:
Harris is, of course, famous for Harris Tweed, and while the industry has declined in recent decades many islanders still rely on the fabric for their livelihood. The island's only tourist information centre at Tarbert has the latest information on Tweed workshops to visit (01859 502 011).

Ardslave, Isle of Harris (opposite); the stunning white sands of Luskentyre on the Island of Taransay (overleaf).

Snow business

❯ CAIRNGORMS, HIGHLANDS

How to get there:

Aviemore is found on the B9152, with the Cairngorm Mountain resort 9 miles to the south east, accessible by road, rail or on foot.

For sat nav users: PH22 1RB

Nearest railway station: Aviemore (9 miles)

Bus services: www.rapsons.co.uk

01463 222 244

Find out more:

www.cairngormmountain.co.uk

01479 861 261

People have enjoyed skiing for pleasure in Scotland since the early 1900s, although most in those days used to ski cross-country rather than downhill. That all changed in the Second World War. During training for winter warfare the troops stationed in Glenmore Lodge near Loch Morlich and Forest Lodge at Abernethy caught the downhill bug. Once war was over many still wanted to strap on skis and hurtle down a slope or two. Over time increasing numbers started to head towards Aviemore and the Cairngorms with their wooden skis in hand. The only problem was that once they had made the difficult hike up the slopes, by the time they were ready to ski back down, night was falling. In 1961, the day before Christmas Eve, winter-sports lovers must have cheered as Scotland's first chairlift opened on Cairngorm Mountain. Suddenly a day on the piste didn't mean aching legs from a lengthy uphill climb.

Before long a five-star hotel appeared at Coylumbridge and in 1966 the Aviemore Centre opened aiming to transform the placid little mountain village into the Zermatt of Scotland. Skiing on Cairngorm reached its heyday in the 1970s with 650,000 Brits heading for the Scottish slopes. While Cairngorm certainly isn't on the scale of European ski-resorts, the mountain still has a licence to thrill when the conditions are right. The best times to ski are generally between February and March although there's always the chance of a decent flurry any time between November and April. Recent cold conditions have even seen Scotland's skiing fortunes begin to pick up after a set of disastrously milder and wetter winters meant snow was an infrequent visitor and holidaymakers headed for the continent. Christmas 2009 was celebrated as the best Cairngorm season for 14 years.

In its attempts to court skiers and snowboarders, the ski-resort opened a funicular railway in 2002. Over a mile long, it conveys holidaymakers to Ptarmigan Station near the summit of the 1,254-metre mountain. After a series of bad seasons, hopes are high that £4 million of new funding will help Cairngorm compete with its European rivals in years to come.

John Craven remembers the Cairngorms ❯❯

The Cairngorms was one of the first locations I ever visited on *Countryfile* and I've returned again and again, spending a lot of time on that famous ski-lift. Walking along the top of Cairngorm is utterly invigorating and even if you're not a skier there's plenty of birdlife to spot, from the ptarmigan with its distinctive white winter plumage to the delightful little snow-bunting.

Not that I could see much on that first journey. We headed up to Scotland in the middle of a blizzard. Luckily I was driving the good old *Countryfile* Land-Rover, one of the first Discoverys in the UK. We carried on even as they were closing the A9, thankful for our four-wheel drive. It was the beginning of a memorable shoot – the helicopter also broke down on the top of the mountain, stranding us as we waited for repairs. Those snow-buntings kept an eye on us though.

Other things to see:
The Cairngorm reindeer are Scotland's only herd of Santa's favourite sledge-pullers. There are visits daily to see the free-ranging herd, weather permitting.
www.reindeer-company.
demon.co.uk
01479 861 228

The ski-lift at Glenshee Ski Centre, Cairnwell (left); a festive resident of the Cairngorm National Park (top).

Lost and found

❯ THE GLENFINNAN MONUMENT, HIGHLANDS

On 19 August 1745, at the head of Loch Shiel, Prince Charles Edward Stuart raised his 5-metre white standard and rallied 1,200 Highlanders to join him in restoring the exiled Stuarts to the throne. The campaign was to end in bloody defeat at Culloden nine months later.

By 1815 the threat of the Jacobite uprisings had passed but to stop Bonnie Prince Charlie's story fading into history, Alexander MacDonald of Glenaladale raised a new kind of standard – a monument commemorating the clansman who had fought for the cause. The unknown highlander, in full battle dress, now watches over the valley and perhaps he saw who made off with Bonnie Prince Charlie's stone.

This weather-worn boulder measuring 30 centimetres in diameter was the very one used to anchor the Prince's standard on that August afternoon, a hole hewn out of the rock so that the staff could slot in. In 1989 the stone mysteriously vanished from its usual knoll near the Monument. After 20 years, historians had begun to give up hope that it would ever be recovered. That was until *Countryfile* came along.

A 79-year-old Hartlepool pensioner, Connie Lofthouse, settled down one Sunday to watch the programme and saw Ben Fogle interviewing local historian Iain Thornber about the missing stone. When a picture flashed up on screen she immediately recognised it – after all, it had been sitting in her rockery for over a decade. Connie had been given the stone while living near Glencoe in 1990 and took it with her when she moved to England two years later. She wrote to the *Countryfile* office in Birmingham and the stone was collected by Mr Thornber. 'I couldn't believe it when I saw it on *Countryfile*,' Connie said at the time. 'I knew straight away that it was my stone, but none of my family believed me at first. It's incredible to think that big part of history has been sat in my garden all this time.'

How to get there:
Take the A830 to Glenfinnan. There is a visitor centre on the main road close to the Monument.
For sat nav users: PH37 4LT
Nearest railway station: Glenfinnan (¼ mile)
Bus services:
www.shielbuses.co.uk
01967 431 272

Find out more:
www.nts.org.uk
0844 493 2221

Glenfinnan Viaduct as the Jacobite Steam Train from Fort William passes through.

Other things to see:
Fans of the Harry Potter films will recognise the curved Glenfinnan Viaduct, the first concrete-built viaduct in the world, as the route Harry takes to Hogwarts. The Hogwart Express is actually the Jacobite Steam Train that travels between Fort William and Mallaig.
www.steamtrain.info
0845 128 4681

The Glenfinnan Monument overlooking Lochshiel.

Rural retreat

▶ LOCH LOMOND AND THE TROSSACHS NATIONAL PARK, WEST DUNBARTONSHIRE

How to get there:

A good place to start exploring the park is the Trossachs Discovery Centre in Aberfoyle, Stirlingshire, on the A821.
For sat nav users: FK8 3UQ
Nearest railway station:
Arrochar & Tarbet (35 miles)
Bus services:
www.travelinescotland.com
0871 200 22 33

Find out more:

www.lochlomond-trossachs.org
08452 255 121

Other things to see:

Set on an island in Lake of Menteith, the stunning Inchmahome Priory once provided safe haven to Mary Queen of Scots and is accessible by ferry from Port of Menteith.

Over the years the Scottish have claimed to have invented many things, from football to Chicken Tikka Masala. However, one of Scotland's own can be credited with the idea of National Parks. John Muir (1838–1914) wrote of 'pristine lands without domesticated animals and free of people'. Ironically, Scotland didn't receive its own National Park until the Loch Lomond and the Trossachs National Park was created in 2002.

Generations of urban Scots have rushed for Loch Lomond when they needed a breath of fresh air. The 24-mile long stretch of water is 600 feet (183 metres) deep and is within an hour's drive for some 70 per cent of Scotland's population. There are currently 1,862 registered speedboats on what has become Glasgow's aquatic playground, with 932 motor cruisers, 769 jet skis, 240 motorboats and one paddle steamer, the *Maid of the Loch*. Although that means that

A winter sunset over the reeds and rushes of Lake of Menteith.

Muir's dream of a people-free environment hasn't quite been realised, elsewhere in the 720 square miles of park, tranquillity is thankfully abundant.

The Trossachs are often described as the Highlands in miniature – and for good reason. Over 1,240 miles of paths criss-cross the romantic land of Sir Walter Scott's *Rob Roy* (1818), taking in 21 of the dramatic Munro mountains and much atmospheric woodland. Some of the finest can be found in the Queen Elizabeth Forest Park, over 20,000 hectares (50,000 acres) of wood, mountain and moorland lying right on top of the Highland boundary fault. Here you can walk in the footsteps of Jacobite rebels around Lake of Menteith (appropriately meaning 'armed to the teeth'), spot kestrel and golden eagle swooping across the still waters of Loch Katrine, or stake out red squirrels from the David Marshall Lodge hide.

The National Park is also going to be the home of a brand-new forest the size of Glasgow of native broadleaf woodland that will support ospreys, voles, otters and woodpeckers. There's only one snag: you'll have to wait 200 years to see it in all its glory. The Great Trossachs Forest is one of Europe's biggest environmental-regeneration schemes and will require the planting of a million new native trees by 2013. Then it will be a case of sitting back and waiting. John Muir would have been overjoyed.

Fit for a queen

▶ GLAMIS CASTLE, ANGUS

How to get there:

Glamis Castle is at Forfar on
the A928, off the A94.

For sat nav users: DD8 1RJ

Nearest railway station:
Dundee (12 miles)

Bus services:

www.travelinescotland.com

0871 200 22 33

Find out more:

www.glamis-castle.co.uk

01307 840 393

Anyone who has stared at a Scottish £10 note, wondering if they can use it in England, has seen Glamis Castle. The fairytale fortress is unusual not only for its romantic trappings but also for the fact that it is set in the fertile Strathmore Valley rather than high on a commanding ridge. The ancestral seat of the Bowes-Lyons since 1372, it was the childhood home of the Queen Mother and the birthplace of Princess Margaret.

The castle's décor changes within the space of a few rooms, highlighting the long history of the building. Its crypt, which never actually housed the dead, is a lower hall that dates back to the medieval period in which the family welcomed visitors. Up the 143-step spiral staircase you'll find the vast drawing room, once the great hall, with its barrel-vaulted ceiling covered with the lions of the Lyons, the roses of England and the thistles of Scotland. The styling changes again when you enter the Royal Apartments, furnished in 1923 by the 13th Countess of Strathmore after her daughter – the future Queen Mother – married Prince Albert, the future George VI. For those seeking a more morbid thrill one of the oldest rooms has been named Duncan's Hall, after the infamous murder of King Duncan by Macbeth, Thane of Glamis, in Shakespeare's Scottish play. The actual deed was done near Elgin – but let's not allow a few historical details to get in the way of a chilling story.

And there have been plenty of those over the years at Glamis. Paranormal experts often name this as one of the most haunted castles in Britain. There's the Grey Lady who haunts the family chapel, possibly the vengeful spirit of Lady Janet Douglas, burnt at the stake as a witch in 1537, and the rather bizarre tongue-less lady who runs around the grounds pointing at her ruined mouth. The macabre menagerie swells with the spectre of a poorly-treated slave-boy and a pair of phantom card-players in the crypt. Most disturbing is the castle's very own monster, allegedly hidden in a secret room. It's more than likely that the legend has spun from the tragic tale of a deformed child born to the family in 1821 and locked away to hide his affliction. In recent years the castle has tried to play down the supernatural reputation it once embraced and dwells instead on its château-like turrets, royal apartments, fine library, arboretum and extensive grounds.

Other things to see:
Highlights of Glamis Castle gardens include its formal Italian Garden, laid out by the Queen Mother's mother, enclosed behind high yew hedges, and a nature trail through huge Douglas firs and hardwoods.

Glamis Castle (left); the Italian Garden in the castle grounds (above).

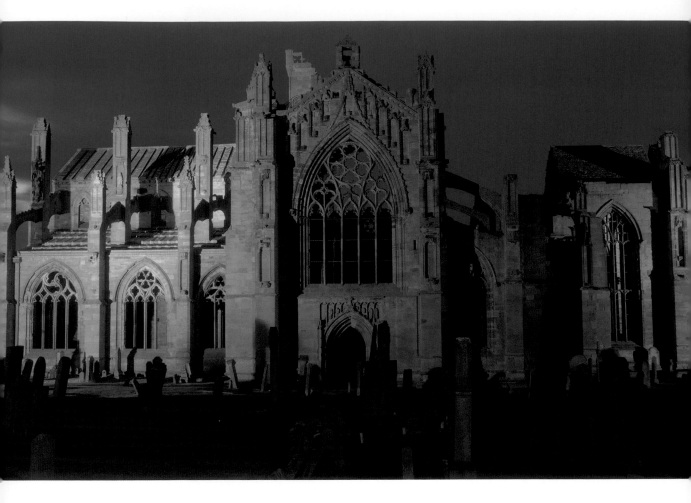

A floodlit Melrose Abbey.

Braveheart

❯ MELROSE ABBEY, SCOTTISH BORDERS

How to get there:

Melrose Abbey is found
off the A6091.
For sat nav users: TD6 9LG
Nearest railway station:
Wallyford (33 miles)
Bus services:
www.firstgroup.com
01324 613 777

You can imagine the excitement on the archaeology site. Historians had been painstakingly excavating the chapter house at Melrose Abbey when they found a small casket beneath 50 centimetres of soil. They immediately realised what they were looking at, as there was evidence that such an object had already been unearthed and reburied in 1921. If they were right, inside the lead casket they would find an older chest containing the mummified heart of Robert the Bruce.

Bruce took the Scottish throne in 1306 and waged the guerrilla war with the English that led to independence in 1327. On his deathbed, Bruce's final wish was that his heart be removed from his body and be carried into battle in the Holy Land. The organ was entrusted to Sir James Douglas, but when the knight was killed in Spain in 1330 it was returned to Scotland and buried at Melrose Abbey.

To confirm its identity, a tiny hole was drilled into the casket and a fibre optic slipped inside. This revealed the second casket alongside a small plaque declaring that the relic did indeed contain a human heart. There is no real way of knowing if it is really Bruce's heart, but examination of the King's corpse in 1818 confirmed that his heart had been removed after death.

The casket received its third burial in a private ceremony and now a stone marks the spot, bearing a line from a 1375 John Barbour poem: 'A noble hart may have nane ease gif freedom failye', which means 'A noble heart can know no ease without freedom.'

Melrose Abbey itself is the third religious house to have been built by the River Tweed. The valley had been occupied by the Romans who established a large fort known as Trimontium (meaning three hills place) and were followed by 7th-century holy men at the Old Melrose chapel, a couple of miles from the present site. In 1131, David I of Scotland gave his blessing for a larger Cistercian abbey, which 200 years later was burnt to the ground by marauding English warriors. The third abbey, which we see today, was built in its place in 1326. The ruins boast astonishingly precise and well-preserved carvings. Saints gaze down while dragons and gargoyles scamper across the stonework and, high above you, on the south side of the nave a gargoyle of a cheeky pig plays bagpipes for all eternity.

Find out more:
www.historic-scotland.gov.uk
01896 822 562

Other things to see:
The Trimontium Exhibition at Newstead reveals the Roman heritage of the area. If it grabs your imagination, there's a three-hour guided tour around the Melrose Roman sites.
For sat nav users: TD6 9PN
www.trimontium.org.uk
01896 822 651

The Common Ridings Cornet with the 'captured' standard.

Joy ride
‣ HAWICK, SCOTTISH BORDERS

The 9th of September 1513 was one of the darkest days in Scottish history. King James IV led an army into England to be met at Flodden in Northumberland by the Earl of Surrey and his men, who surrounded the Scots. By the following day the King and a third of his army were dead – around 17,000 men. Almost every family in Scotland lost someone on that battlefield. Realising that Scotland was on its knees the Earl of Surrey sent half of his men home and the remainder over the border to plunder, leaving towns razed to the ground and crops destroyed. Border communities faced a winter of famine and disease.

Hawick was one town that lost most of its men at Flodden and so reacted with fear when its people heard that an English raiding party had arrived 2 miles away at Hornshole. Knowing that the town wouldn't survive an attack, the remaining young men of Hawick jumped on their horses and without knowing how many soldiers they would meet, rode to Hornshole armed with whatever they

How to get there:
Hawick is found on the A7
Edinburgh to Carlisle.
For sat nav users: TD9
Nearest railway station:
Lockerbie (48 miles)
Bus services:
www.firstgroup.com
08708 72 72 71

Find out more:
www.hawickcommonriding.com
01450 378 853

Other things to see:
The Hawick Horse Monument
commemorates the bravery
of those original lads who
protected the town against
raiders. Bizarrely most locals call
the horse 'Ken' after the habit
of using the horse as the basis
of road directions. Ask where
anything is and you'll probably
be asked: 'Dive ee ken the horse?'
meaning 'Do you know where
the horse is?'

'Ken', the Hawick Horse
Monument.

could find. Amazingly, taking the English by surprise, these few brave lads managed to defeat
them, returning to Hawick victorious, holding the flag of the vanquished English high.

Every year Hawick celebrates the tale with the Common Ridings. The festivities start in
May, when the year's Cornet, the honoured soul who leads the procession, is chosen. There
have been Cornets elected every year since 1703, an unbroken line other than during the
two world wars when the festival was cancelled. Over the following weeks the Cornet and his
supporters ride out to the surrounding farms and villages, culminating with a 24-mile ride to
Mosspaul and back.

The main celebrations kick off one Friday morning in June. At 6am sharp the Drum and
Fife Band blast the town awake to enjoy the delights of rum and milk before breakfast, while
packets of snuff are thrown from upstairs windows to the crowd below. Then 300 men mount
their steeds and process around the town before heading to Nipknowles to gallop up the
hill after the Cornet, who is proudly clutching the captured standard. An evening of balls and
feasts awaits them on their return to Hawick, and the following day the flag is ceremoniously
returned to the Council Chambers.

The magic hill
▶ ELECTRIC BRAE, AYRSHIRE

Every year people flock to a small section of the A719 between Dunure and Croy Bay, get out of their cars and marvel. There's no ancient monument or castle to see. There's no extraordinary wildlife to witness. There's not even lashings of Scottish history to hand. So why head to this seemingly empty scrap of countryside?

The answer comes when you step out of your car, making sure you've left the handbrake off and out of gear. There, in front of your amazed eyes your vehicle will begin to roll, ever so slowly up the hill. The bizarre phenomenon came to public attention during the Second World War when US personnel serving at Prestwick Airport rushed to see gravity being foxed by a simple road. Even General Eisenhower broke off from official military matters to pop over and gape. But what was behind the marvel that became known as the Electric Brae?

These days the explanation can be found on a cairn by the road. The sensation of rolling up is due to an optical illusion. The section of road has a slope of 1 in 86 heading upwards. However, the land on either side of the road lies in such a way that your brain interprets the incline as running in the opposite direction. So, when cars are rolling down the hill, they look like they're climbing. The funny thing is that even when you know the secret of the Electric Brae, you still can't help but be deceived by it. Just remember that you are on a public road; you won't be able to pass off allowing your car to roll into another as an optical illusion.

How to get there:

The Electric Brae is found on the A719 near Dunure. Nearest railway station: Maybole (6 miles) There is no bus service.

Find out more:

www.ayrshire-arran.com
0845 22 55 121

The poetic ruins of Dunure Castle.

Other things to see:

There is of course much more to Arran than bad football – the eerie Machrie Moor stone circles on the west of the island, for example. Its slabs of red sandstone are believed to have been erected in 1800 BC.

Stone circle at Machrie Moor, Isle of Arran.

The coast around the Electric Brae is also worth exploring. The fishing village of Dunure, just north of the Brae, has a romantic 13th-century castle. You are also rewarded with lovely views of the Isle of Arran. This beautiful island is almost like Scotland in miniature, offering you the chance to experience the country's changing landscapes within just a few short miles. It also has the honour of being the home of the world's worst football club. Northend Thistle, of Lochranza, hasn't won a game in 18 years. The captain blames their lack of success on the fact that the town only has a population of 200 and 150 of those are retired.

Wildlife stronghold

▶ CAERLAVEROCK CASTLE AND NATURE RESERVE, DUMFRIES AND GALLOWAY

How to get there:

Caerlaverock Castle is located south east of Dumfries on the B725.
For sat nav users: DG1 4RU
Nearest railway station: Dumfries (8 miles)
Bus services: www.stagecoachbus.com/western
01292 613 500

Seen from the air Caerlaverock Castle is unique, forming a near perfect triangle with its three formidable battlements, two towers, gatehouse and double moat. It is believed that the castle was originally built by the Maxwell family and was a peaceful place until Edward I invaded. Such a stronghold couldn't be ignored by English forces and in 1300 Lord Maxwell surrendered during a violent siege of 87 knights and 3,000 men. For the next 12 years the castle was an English base of operations until its commander switched sides and pledged his allegiance to Robert the Bruce. In 1314, Bruce commanded that all castles along the border be demolished to stop them being used by future invading armies. Caerlaverock was razed to the ground, only to be rebuilt in the 15th century, with extensive Renaissance-style lodgings added in the 1630s. Just a few years later, the castle would find itself under siege once more, as protestant Covenanters surrounded the Catholic castle for 12 weeks. Ultimately triumphant, the religious rebels stormed the fort and laid waste to it. Today its ruins, while a little off the beaten track, are a kids' favourite, with an adventure park and siege museum.

Caerlaverock means 'castle of the lark' and appropriately is now the home to a 546-hectare (1,350-acre) national nature reserve, one mile east. In autumn this mudflat and salt-marsh habitat is transformed into a wildlife spectacle as 12,000 migrating barnacle geese swoop in

between October–November. By December, the numbers reach their zenith as the birds build up their reserves ready for the 2,000-mile return trip to the Arctic to breed. After a day gorging themselves on farmland roots and seeds they will flock back to the mudflats for the night.

This is a real conservation success story. In the 1940s the Solway Firth only hosted around 500 overwintering barnacle geese. Today, more than 25,000 can make the reserve their temporary home.

Other things to see:

New Abbey is a small, one-street village 15 miles from Caerlaverock, nestling beside the ruins of Sweetheart Abbey. Its unusual name comes from its founder, Devorgilla de Balliol (1220–90), who founded the monastery in memory of her dead husband. So besotted was Devorgilla that she carried his embalmed heart with her for 22 years until her own death. www.historic-scotland.gov.uk 01387 850 397

Find out more:

Castle:
www.historic-scotland.gov.uk
01387 770 244
Nature reserve:
www.org.uk/visit-us/caerlaverock
01387 770 200

An aerial view of Caerlaverock Castle shows the fortresses' near perfect triangular construction.

Wales

Wales is the birthplace of British tourism. In the 18th century romantic poets, artists and writers took to the Principality, most notably the lush Wye Valley, on the British equivalent of the European Grand Tour. These pioneers of the picturesque spawned the tourist industry that now supports many rural industries and kicked off a publishing revolution of guide books and travel guides, much like the one you're holding in your hands right now.

What would they have made of modern Wales? They would have appreciated the glories of Snowdonia, but probably would have been amazed to find a tea-room at Snowdon's peak. Heads would be scratched about the seemingly crazy pastime of coasteering – it's hard to imagine Wordsworth or Turner throwing themselves off a cliff – but they would have been heartened that the wonders of Welsh castles like Carreg Cennen still rub shoulders with more modern marvels such as Pontcysyllte Aqueduct. Did these early tourists stand entranced as dolphins played off Cardigan Bay or watched hares box in the Tanat Valley? And whatever would they make of mountain-bike bog snorkelling? Some aspects of modern tourism may not be to the refined tastes of old, but one thing is certain – every visitor to Wales, both ancient and modern, can't help falling in love with the place.

Tea with the gods
❯ SNOWDON, SNOWDONIA

Devil's Bridge Waterfall (previous page); the peak of Mount Snowdon and the valley of Snowdonia (above).

In 1935 the first cup of tea was served from what was then the highest building in England, Scotland and Wales. The Snowdon Café, designed by Sir Clough Williams-Ellis, creator of the nearby resort village of Portmeirion, lies 1,085 metres above sea level. The café was in essence a concrete bunker, perhaps deserving of the damnation heaped upon it when Prince Charles dubbed it 'the highest slum in Wales'.

All that changed in 2009. Despite extreme weather conditions – temperatures down to -20°C and windspeeds of 150mph, which regularly meant that the only way up and down the ice-laden mountain for the 80-plus construction force was on foot – a brand-new visitor centre and café opened. Named Hafod Eryri, which roughly translates as 'Summer residence on Snowdonia'), the building project often faced controversy, not least because its steel structure is faced with Portuguese stone rather than local Welsh rock. The sad fact is that it is cheaper to transport stone from the continent than quarry it from the foot of Mount Snowdon itself. To calm the storm this decision whipped up, more expensive granite from Cwt Y Bugail quarry near Blaenau Ffestiniog was brought in to complete the walls.

In an earlier age, access to the top was another source of controversy. You can make the ascent up Snowdon on foot or mountain bike, but most people let the train take the strain. In the early 19th century, holiday makers used to don hiking boots or jump on the back of a donkey. The railway revolution offered an easier way to reach the summit but construction was at first foiled at every turn by the local landowner, George William Duff Assheton Smith. For 20 years he rejected one proposal after another for fear that a line would spoil Snowdonia's spectacular scenery. Finally, faced with a rival plan to build a railway on the other side of the mountain, he relented and the Snowdon Mountain Railway, the highest in the British Isles, opened in 1896. At first, two hotels greeted passengers making the trip to the top but after one was literally blown off the side of the mountain, the other went bankrupt in the 1930s.

Rack-and-pinion mountain trains leave from Llanberis station five miles below, taking in ineffable views as steam or diesel engines shunt the carriages ever higher at 5mph. For a brew with a view it's a journey worth making and, as the verse carved on to the side of Hafod Eryri affirms: 'You are nearer to heaven.'

Other things to see:

After the natural splendour of Snowdon, take an electrifying trip to an industrial marvel, the massive hydro-electrical power station of Dinorwig, deep within the Elidir Fawr mountain on the edge of the Snowdonia National Park.
www.electricmountain.co.uk
01286 870 636

How to get there:
The Snowdon Mountain Railway is at Llanberis on the A4086. Weather permitting, trains run daily from late Mar–Oct but the summit can only be reached between mid-June and the end of the season.
For sat nav users: LL55 4TY
Nearest railway station:
Bangor (11½ miles)
Bus services:
www.traveline.info
0871 200 22 33

Find out more:

www.snowdonrailway.co.uk
0844 493 8120

A more leisurely way to reach the top of Snowdon.

Walking on the shoulders of giants
▶ THE PRECIPICE WALK, SNOWDONIA

According to a local legend, anyone who spends the night atop the brooding 893-metre high mountain of Cadair Idris will wake either a poet or stark raving mad. For some, the very thought of climbing such a precipitous peak is insanity but a ramble on footpaths through the nearby Nannau estate does offer even the most casual walker the chance to experience majestic views of the Mawddach Estuary. Described as 'sublime' by William Wordsworth, who felt it would 'compare with the finest in Scotland', the estuary was once the domain of gold speculators who panned along the entire length of the river, and has also been used as an artillery range in its time. Now that both gold and guns have passed it by, the estuary is a fertile mixture of wood and wetland, interspersed with the odd sandy beach. It is an exceptional place at both dawn and dusk.

Despite its scary-sounding name, the four-mile Precipice Walk on the lower slopes of Foel Cynwch can get a little narrow at times but involves hardly any climbing, although at 244 metres it is probably best not attempted by vertigo sufferers. Other than a couple of stiles to hop over, the path can be enjoyed by any sure-footed walker aged eight or 80.

Travel anticlockwise around the circular route and the mountains of Moelwyn and Snowdon rise up to the north while a heather-clad Rhinog looms to the west. Dare to look down and the land around Mawddach Estuary, though impressive, is relatively tamed. When the Romans arrived in Britain this was dense, intraversable jungle, dominated by swamps and vegetation. No wonder prehistoric man took to high mountain paths, skirting the treetops in safety. If a saunter along Precipice Walk is spectacular today, imagine what it would have been like for our earliest ancestors.

How to get there:
The circular Precipice Walk starts from the car park off the A498 Dolgellau to Bala road. Nearest railway station: Morfa Mawddach (8 miles) Bus services: www.traveline-cymru.info 0871 200 22 33

Find out more:
www.visitmidwales.co.uk 01654 703 526

Other things to see:
The Mawddach Estuary is also home to an RSPB nature reserve, featuring a number of trails, including one suitable for wheelchair users. Buzzards and ravens take to the air no matter what time of year you visit, but in spring the estuary becomes a haven for pied flycatchers, redstarts and wood warblers. Access is free. www.rspb.org.uk 01341 442 071

A view from the Precipice Walk, looking south-west over the Mawddach Valley and Afon Mawddach (opposite); the Mawddach Estuary (overleaf).

Towering achievement

▶ PONTCYSYLLTE AQUEDUCT, WREXHAM

How to get there:

Take the A539 to Whitchurch
and Llangollen, following signs
to Pontcysyllte Aqueduct.
Nearest railway station:
Chirk (4 miles)
Bus services:
www.arrivabus.co.uk
0871 200 22 33

Find out more:

www.visitwales.co.uk
08708 300 306

Other things to see:

The small town of Llangollen
is swamped with visitors from
all around the world every July,
for the annual International
Musical Eisteddfod. Over 5,000
singers, musicians and dancers
from 50 countries perform over
a period of six days.
www.llangollen.org.uk
01978 860 828

A canal boat travelling
over Pontcysyllte
Aqueduct, along the
Shropshire Union Canal
(above); Devil's Bridge
and the more sturdy
iron bridge, which was
built over the second
stone bridge in 1901
(opposite).

Thomas Telford and William Jessop had a
problem. The canal they were building to
link the coalmines of Denbighshire with the
national canal system, the lifeblood of the
Industrial Revolution, ran through the Dee
Valley, with a sudden drop of 38 metres.

The two legendary engineers' solution
became a UNESCO World Heritage Site
in 2009, a recognition that puts the
Pontcysllte Aqueduct in the same league
as such landmarks as the Great Wall of
China, the Taj Mahal and Stonehenge. Work
began on the project in July 1795 and the
aqueduct officially opened ten years later.
Unfortunately, costs had spiralled to a total
of £45,000. Ironically the overspend meant
that the entire canal system ran out of
money before it could be completed and
had to finish prematurely at the Trevor Basin,
a quarter of a mile from the aqueduct.

Pontcysyllte means 'the bridge that
connects the river'. Spanning the valley from Trevor to Froncysyllte, with the River Dee roaring
beneath, the aqueduct consists of 18 piers and 19 arches, each with a 14-metre span. More
than 10,000 boats now cross the aqueduct every year, travelling along a 307-metre long
trough, which is just wider that the vessels themselves. Astoundingly, this narrow trough
holds 1.5 million litres of water.

The biggest concern for the engineers was the weight of the structure because they
wanted the aqueduct to appear as graceful as possible. Instead of using stone throughout,
the workmen constructed the arches from two-centimetre thick cast-iron plates. To make
it lighter still while maintaining flexibility the trough itself wasn't bolted down but held in
place by the sheer weight of the water.

Crossing the bridge by either boat or foot is an unforgettable experience, although with
only one handrail on the towpath; if you want to join the 25,000 pedestrians who make use
of the bridge every year, you'll need a strong head for heights.

Work of the devil
› DEVIL'S BRIDGE FALLS, CEREDIGION

Three bridges rack up one above the other at the exact spot where the River Mynach drops 90 metres to greet the River Rheidol below. The lowest and oldest bridge is said to have been raised by Satan himself. The story goes that an old crone was walking through the valley when her cow became stranded on the other side of the gorge. Hearing her cry for help, the Devil appeared, offering to build her a bridge so that the beast could be rescued. The toll for the bridge would be the soul of the first living creature to walk across it. She solemnly agreed but when the last stone was laid she threw a crust of bread across the chasm. Her mangy dog chased after the loaf and on crossing the bridge became the property of Satan. Cursing, the Devil vanished, never to return, embarrassed that he had been outsmarted by an old woman.

The original name for the site gives you a clue of who really built the bridge. Pontarfynach means 'monk's bridge' and was actually designed as part of a trade route for 11th-century Cistercian monks from nearby Strata Florida Abbey. The second stone bridge was built in the 1700s when the first was deemed too perilous for carriages, with the third – made of iron – erected in 1901 to handle modern traffic.

The waterfall has been an attraction since Victorian times and there are two ways to explore it. The first is a quite strenuous clamber down 100 steep, narrow steps, while the second is a far easier route around the Devil's Punchbowl at the bottom of the fall.

Find out more:
www.devilsbridgefalls.co.uk
01970 890 233

Other things to see:
The Vale of Rheidol Railway was originally opened to transport silver and lead from the mines to Aberystwyth. Today, you can board the train at either Aberystwyth or Pontarfynach, taking in views of the Rheidol on the way.
www.rheidolrailway.co.uk
01970 625 819

How to get there:
Devil's Bridge Falls is found on the A4120, west of Aberystwyth.
For sat nav users: SY23 3JW
Nearest railway station: Aberystwycth (12 miles)
Bus services:
www.traveline.org.uk
0871 200 22 33

John Craven on dolphin watching »

The whole of Cardigan Bay is magnificent. I've been there many times for *Countryfile*, exploring the connections with the poet Dylan Thomas from the house in which he used to live to the pubs he used to frequent. (Actually, I think that's most of the pubs on the Bay.)

Then there are the dolphins. The first time I was there to report on the dolphins I pulled back the curtains in my hotel bedroom to see them already playing in the bay at eight o'clock in the morning. Almost immediately we were out in a boat with a whole school leaping around us. I've never seen so many dolphins in UK waters. One of the best experiences in 20 years of *Countryfile*.

Unexpected visitors
▶ CARDIGAN BAY, CEREDIGION

How to get there:

The village of New Quay is found at the end of the A486. For sat nav users: SA45 9NZ Nearest railway station: Fishguard Harbour (21 miles) Bus services: www.traveline.org.uk 0871 200 22 33

Find out more:

www.visitcardigan.com 01239 613 230

Think of Welsh animals and the first that come to mind will almost certainly be sheep. Yet stand on the west coast and you've got every chance of seeing something you more likely connect with Florida.

Cardigan Bay is one of the two places around Britain that is home to some of the largest bottlenose dolphins on earth; the other being the Moray Firth in Scotland. Twice as long as a grown man and eight times his weight, dolphins are now living in the bay, attracted by the salmon that migrate back to the rivers to spawn. These highly sociable mammals behave pretty much the same way as humans when they get together, forming groups as they travel. Some individuals prefer small clusters while other, more gregarious souls form larger crowds. Some even appear to flit between gangs, possibly passing on information and seeming to glue the groups together. One thing is certain – all bottlenose dolphins like to play, and can be regularly seen leaping from the water from the Dyfi Estuary to Cardigan itself. However, those in the know say that your best chance of a sighting is just south of Cardigan between April and September. Spy a crowd forming at the ancient fishing village of New Quay, and it's a fair bet that dolphins have made an appearance, swimming near the harbour wall. You may even be lucky enough to also witness common dolphins, Atlantic grey seals, porpoises and whales within these waters. Spotting the dolphins in Cardigan Bay isn't too difficult but if you want to increase your chances here's some pointers. While they can be seen at most times of the day, you'll probably have more luck during early mornings or evenings when there is more boat traffic. Calm, sunny days give you the best conditions and you'll usually catch more activity around high tide.

Bottlenose dolphins in Cardigan Bay.

The lookout shelter on Bird Rock.

Remember that Cardigan Bay is a European Special Area of Conservation and the dolphins themselves are a protected species. If you hanker for a closer encounter and take a boat into the bay, it's important to maintain a steady speed or slow down gradually as soon as you spot dolphin activity. And whatever you do, don't chase or attempt to feed the dolphins. Just sit back and marvel as some of nature's most graceful creatures play right in front of you.

Other things to see:

The Cardigan Bay Lookout Shelter on Bird Rock near New Quay is a refurbished coastguard's hut offering stunning panoramic views of the coastline and handy identification boards to help you pick out the local birdlife, including Britain's rarest crow, the chough, as well as razorbills and guillemots.

The saint and the hares

❯ ST MELANGELL'S CHURCH, POWYS

Melangell was, legend has it, an Irish princess who fled her father's court to escape marriage to a man she didn't love. A pious woman, she settled into the life of a hermit in the Tanat Valley for some fifteen years. Then, in AD 604, the venerable Prince Brochwell Ysgithrog of Powys was hunting hares with a pack of hounds. Suddenly their prey vanished. The animals were found sheltering under the robes of Melangell who was kneeling in prayer among the brambles. Moved by her spirituality, the Prince dismounted his steed and offered Melangell the valley in which to establish a sanctuary for both man and beast. By order of the Prince, hunting was immediately banned in the area. If you were caught chasing a hare, the medieval equivalent of hunt saboteurs would intervene, sending the creature on its way with a cry of 'God and Melangell be with thee'. The holy woman later became the tutelary saint of hares and Celtic patron of all wild animals.

Melangell's bones rest in the blue-grey church that reputedly stands on the spot where the prince found her, encircled by 2,000-year-old yew trees. Pilgrims still visit the Romanesque shrine, the oldest in Britain, 14 centuries after her death. The church itself, founded in the 7th century, became the local place of worship for nearby farmers but now stands alone, as solitary and remote as the woman to whom it is dedicated. And who knows? As you sit in silence, hardly troubled by another living soul in the tightly packed churchyard, you may see the unmistakable flash of a hare darting past.

How to get there:
The Saint Melangell centre is at Pennant Melangell, Llangynog, and is accessible from the B4391 via a single-track road. For sat nav users: SY10 0HQ Nearest railway station: Welshpool (23 miles) There is no bus service.

Find out more:
www.st-melangell.org.uk
01691 860 408

Other things to see:
The Tanat Valley, also known as Gwely y Gawres or 'the Bed of the Giantess', was the stuff of legend long before Melangell's time. No one has ever been able to explain the presence of what is probably a large whale bone that was discovered on the mountainside between Bala and Pennant Melangell; the so-called Giant's Rib is still on display in St Melangell's.

The 12th-century shrine of St Melangell.

Into the depths

▶ NATIONAL SHOWCAVES CENTRE FOR WALES, POWYS

By the light of a flickering candle Tommy Morgan drew an arrow in the sand at his feet. In front of him, his brother Jeff was already striding forward into the gloom. His heart hammering in his chest, Tommy wondered for the umpteenth time whether this had been such a good idea. The brothers had known about the moss-covered cave at Dan-yr-Ogof for years, but no one had ever summoned the courage to explore its tenebrous depths. Yet here they were, stumbling into the darkness with only candles to light their way. At least the arrows in the sand would guide them back. Setting his jaw, Tommy started after Jeff, taking some comfort from the fact that they had brought a revolver with them, just in case.

The Morgan brothers made it back to the surface later that day in 1912. They would return to explore the four subterranean lakes they'd discovered, only to be foiled by a tiny passage that they couldn't push themselves through. It was another 51 years before Eileen Davies of the South Wales Caving Club succeeded where the brothers had failed.

One of the impressive caverns inside the National Showcaves Centre for Wales.

How to get there:
The showcaves are found on
the A4067, exit at Junction 45
from the M4.
For sat nav users: SA9 1GJ
Nearest railway station:
Llangadog (28 miles)
Bus services:
www.traveline-cymru.info
0871 200 22 33

Find out more:
www.showcaves.co.uk
01639 730 284

Other things to see:
Sgwd Y Eira, the 'waterfall of
snow', is near Ystradfellte, one
of Wales's favourite walking
spots. While this is only one of
the many waterfalls you'll find
in the region, a path takes you
behind the roaring waters –
an unforgettable experience.
www.breconbeacons.org
01874 623 366

Thankfully, visitors to the carboniferous-limestone Dan-yr-Ogof showcaves today don't
have to squeeze through the same narrow gap to share what the Morgans and Eileen Davies
found – there's now an entrance through a mined passage.

You've probably seen stalactites and stalagmites that grow down or up respectively but
what about helictites? These delicate formations begin life as tiny stalactites but change their
axis from the vertical, possibly as a result of capillary action, and seemingly defy gravity in
achieving curving or angular shapes. Reaching out sideways like delicate fingers, these bizarre
formations are just some of the underground treats that await you as you walk towards the
Dome of St Paul's, a suitably grand name for a cathedral of a chamber. The emerald water
of the subterranean lake is maintained by twin waterfalls cascading 12 metres from the
ceiling of the cave, while in neighbouring Bone Cave more than 42 human skeletons were
discovered, some of which are still scattered on the chamber's floor.

The showcaves are a safe way to explore just a small part of the geological heritage of the
region. The 11-mile Dan-yr-Ogof system is just part of the Fforest Fawr Geopark, established
by UNESCO in 2005, that celebrates the 470 million years of history found beneath your feet
as you take in the glorious scenery of the Brecon Beacons.

The 'waterfall of snow',
Sgwd Y Eira.

Bog off
❯ LLANWRTYD WELLS, POWYS

How to get there:
Llanwrtyd Wells is on the A483.
For sat nav users: LD5 4RB
(tourist information centre)
Nearest railway station:
Llanwrtyd (1 mile)
Bus services:
www.traveline.info
0871 200 22 33

Find out more:
www.llanwrtyd.com
01591 610 666

Other things to see:
Ten miles up the A483 you'll find Cilmery, a pretty little village with a monumental reputation. It was here, in 1282, that the last Welsh prince of Wales, Llywelyn ap Gruffydd, was slain after a chance meeting with Edward I's forces. The soldiers didn't even realise whom they had killed until after he'd breathed his regal last. Look for the memorial erected near the spot where he died. For sat nav users: LD2

Once upon a time Llanwrtyd Wells' only claim to fame was that, with a population of 600, it was the smallest town in Britain. Now, its reputation is a little – how shall we say this – weirder.

It's all the town's own doing though, thanks to the series of crackpot festivals that fills its calendar. For the thousands who flock here every year to watch, or participate in, the bizarre goings-on, the phenomenal scenery of this ancient volcanic region is just the backdrop to the real action.

The year kicks off with the Saturnalia Wobble in January, a mountain-biking and beer festival, in which the bikers don Roman fancy dress. Why? Just because, that's why. Then in June comes the Man vs Horse Marathon, which is as bonkers as it sounds. It was the first of Llanwrtyd Wells' crazy capers to be organised by then landlord of the Neuadd Arms, Gordon Green, in 1980. Ben Fogle was sent by *Countryfile* to compete in 2008, but couldn't come close to the record set by Huw Lobb who finally managed to beat an equine rival by two minutes over the hilly 22-mile course.

Competitors in the Man vs Horse Marathon.

One month later it's time to don swimming goggles with the Bog Snorkelling Triathlon, in which you run 12 miles, plunge into a 197-foot (60-metre) trench of muddy water and then top it all off with a 25-mile mountain-bike ride. The World Mountain Bike Bog Snorkelling Championship takes things a step further. Instead of swimming through the mire, you attempt to ride a mountain bike through it. To help you in your absurd endeavours the bespoke bikes provided have their tyres filled with water and lead weights fore and aft. If you think riding one of these on dry land is difficult, it's near impossible in the drink.

Thankfully, there are a few slightly tamer activities on offer. The June Drovers Walk follows in the footsteps of the farmers of yesteryear who used to trudge their geese, cattle and sheep huge distances to markets, while the Saturnalia Ramble in January gives you a chance to walk off your Christmas excesses through the Welsh winter wonderland. Togas are optional.

Bog snorkelling – one of a number of unusual competitions held annually in Llanwrtyd Wells.

John Craven on the Gower Peninsula ››

We've visited the Gower Peninsula many, many times over the last 20 years of *Countryfile*, but I never mind. It's simply beautiful, for which reason it became Britain's first Area of Outstanding Natural Beauty, designated in 1956. The journey there leads you through some pretty industrial areas but once you leave Swansea you find yourself on some of the best beaches Britain has to offer. I'm no surfer, but watching the dramatic waves break on a hot summer's day I can see why the beaches of Three Cliffs Bay and Llangennith are so attractive to surfing fans. The most popular beach is probably the 3-mile long Rhossili Bay, where you get a fantastic sunset over the Worm's Head, the limestone islet that snakes out into the sea.

Welsh pride
❯ CARREG CENNEN CASTLE, CARMARTHENSHIRE

How to get there:

The castle is found via minor roads from the A483 near Trapp Village.

For sat nav users: SA19 6TS

Nearest railway station: Llandybie (3 miles)

There is no bus service.

Find out more:

www.cadw.wales.gov.uk

01443 336 000

Other things to see:

The castle's Cliff Gallery, a passageway cut into the cliff face, leads down to a pitch-black cave that can only be explored by torchlight. The sacred wishing well found within the narrow cavern was once said to cure ear and eye disorders.

Owain Lawgoch (of the Red Hand) was a 14th-century Welsh prince who fought alongside the French in the Hundred Years War. A skilled fighter, he was such a threat to the English that they had an English spy stab him in the back during the siege of the castle in the French town of Mortagne, north of Bordeaux, in 1378. Local folk tales insist that he lies asleep beneath Carreg Cennen Castle waiting for the call to rise and claim his rightful throne.

Owain couldn't have chosen a more dramatic place for an extended nap. This isolated 100-metre limestone crag above the River Cennen has been a home to man since before Roman times. The first mention of a castle in this remote spot comes in 1248 when Rhys Fychan was forced to retake his family home after his mother had simply handed it over to the Normans just to spite her son. The wildly romantic ruin that now stands in its place dates from the 13th century, most likely built by John Giffard of Brimpsfield after he was given the land by a victorious Edward I.

Reaching the castle today means a bracing ascent, so imagine what it must have been like for anyone trying to launch an attack back in the 13th century. The view that greets you when you finally reach the castle walls is staggering – a sweeping vista of the Black Mountains.

But reaching the top of the hill was quite literally only half the battle. The only way to reach the gatehouse was to make your way over a zig-zagging series of bridges across deep ravines – bridges that could be pulled from beneath your feet at any moment.

It's a testament to Carreg Cennen's location that its current ruinous state wasn't due to a mighty assault. The castle underwent extensive restoration after Welsh rebel leader Owain Glyndwr's revolts in the15th century, but eventually became the refuge for routed Lancastrians during the War of the Roses. After the castle had been abandoned, a 500-strong army of Yorkist workmen set about wrecking the place so that no other Lancastrians could seek shelter within its battlements.

The birthplace of tourism
❯ TINTERN ABBEY, MONMOUTHSHIRE

Find out more:

www.cadw.wales.gov.uk

01291 689 251

If you've ever meandered alongside any of the 44 miles of the River Wye from Chepstow Castle to Hereford then you're in good company. Over time, the likes of Coleridge, Wordsworth, Thackeray and Turner have all ambled through its valley, finding inspiration to translate the verdant landscape into prose, print and paintings. They may have done so with a certain book in their hands. Reverend William Gilpin (1724–1804) wore many hats – clergyman, headmaster, writer and artist – but they combined into his true passion. Gilpin was the father of all British sightseers, a pioneer in the simple pleasure of just sitting back and admiring the view. His 1782 book, *Observations on the River Wye*, transformed this little-known backwater into Britain's very first tourist trap. 'The beauty of these scenes arises chiefly from two circumstances,' Gilpin wrote, 'the lofty banks of the river and its mazy course.'

Both the banks and the course of the river remain although Gilpin may have balked at the constant thrum of traffic that the valley experiences today. It is somewhat ironic that Gilpin himself was more than a little dismissive about one of the valley's principal landmarks, the outstanding ruin of Tintern Abbey. Founded in 1131 by the Cistercians, and then rebuilt in Gothic glory one hundred years later, the once overgrown remains prompted William Wordsworth to ruminate on the true nature of beauty in his 1798 poem, 'Lines Composed a Few Miles above Tintern Abbey'. Yet to Gilpin the shattered monastery was more than a little 'ill-shaped'. He even went so far as to make suggestions as to how the abbey's appearance could be improved by judicious use of a large mallet.

As you stand in the roofless nave of the grand abbey, with a carpet of lush turf beneath your feet, staring at the steep, rising valley walls through the gigantic stone windows frames, the thought of a 18th-century reverend taking a hammer to these ancient stones seems like heresy. Nestled in breathtaking surroundings, this imposing relic of faith and contemplation is, despite Gilpin's opinion, the pinnacle of picturesque panoramas.

Other things to see:

From its lofty position 150 metres above sea level, the top of Symonds Yat Rock offers dazzling views over the serpentine Wye. Birdwatchers keen to witness the fastest creature on earth – the peregrine falcon – can take advantage of the team of RSPB volunteers on hand seven days a week throughout summer, armed with high-spec telescopes and a wealth of knowledge.

The spectacular ruins of Tintern Abbey (right); the view from Symonds Yat Rock overlooking the River Wye as it runs through Herefordshire (overleaf).

How to get there:

The abbey is beside the A466 Chepstow to Monmouth road. For sat nav users: NP16 6TE (Anchor hotel, next to abbey) Nearest railway station: Chepstow (6 miles) Bus services: www.stagecoachbus.com 01452 527 516

Northern Ireland

Breathe in the air of the Emerald Isle and it feels as if you're taking in a lungful of history. This is an ancient place. Of course, mention Northern Ireland and many immediately think of the events of the latter half of the 20th century. This is slowly changing and now more and more people are beginning to explore the delights the country has to offer. Every year thousands flock to marvel at the Giant's Causeway, although there is so much more to Northern Ireland than that. There are the majestic Mountains of Mourne, the front-runner in the race to become Northern Ireland's first National Park, and the natural splendour that is County Fermanagh, said by many to be Northern Ireland's Lake District.

There's a bright future for Northern Ireland too. The largest sea lough in the British Isles, Strangford Lough, is home to an innovative new power plant that is leading the way in green energy, while new driving, walking and canoeing leisure routes are opening up the stunning landscape like never before. There's never been a better time to visit.

Of learned and holy men

❯ DEVENISH ISLAND, COUNTY FERMANAGH

How to get there:

Take the A32 north from
Enniskillen and after 3½
miles, take the B82 to Trory.
A ferry runs from Trory Point
to Devenish every day, Good
Friday–Sept.
For sat nav users: BT94 1PP
(Trory Point)
Nearest railway station: Carrick-
on-Shannon (41 miles)
Bus services:
www.translink.co.uk
028 9066 6630

Find out more:

www.ni-environment.gov.uk
028 6862 1588

Other things to see:

Many pre-Christian idols
were reused by the early Irish
churches and one, the Bishop's
Stone at Killadeas, some
6 miles north of Enniskillen,
is of particular interest. It
features a pagan figure on one
face and the faded outline of a
Christian bishop with crozier
on the other.

Saint Molaise could daydream for Ireland, were it one of the Olympic games. The story goes that the celebrated saint came to Ireland in the 6th century and founded a monastic house on Devenish, the largest of several holy islands in Lough Erne. One morning, the saint took a moment from the hard work of building the monastery to sit down and catch his breath. All at once he became aware of the glorious birdsong around him. Convinced that the Holy Spirit was speaking to him, Molaise was caught up in ecstatic reverie. When the spell finally broke, he brushed himself down and stood up to return to his work, only to find that a century had passed and the monastery had been built around him.

The monastery survived until it was destroyed by fire during a Viking raid in 1157, to be replaced by a later Oratory, the walls of which can be seen today. It is accompanied by a 30-metre high round tower, which probably dates from the 12th century. There are 65 of these towers scattered across Ireland, some topped with a conical cap and usually sited beside an early church. No one really knows why they were built. They could have been watchtowers, although one of the more outlandish theories is that they were intended to collect magnetic radiation from the sun and channel it down to monks meditating within. Others believe that they were used as giant sundials, helping to calculate the longest and shortest days of the year so that Easter and Christmas could be celebrated. Whatever their purpose, if you climb the internal staircase of the Devenish tower, you are rewarded with some amazing views.

The Oratory of Molaise wasn't the only religious house on Devenish. This 5-hectare (12-acre) island also houses Teampull Mor, a 13th-century church with a striking moulded south window, and St Mary's Augustinian Priory atop the island's hill. Best preserved of all of Devenish's holy buildings, this 15th- or 16th-century church includes an unusual, freestanding, intricate stone cross in its graveyard.

Today the island is known for its Christian heritage, but historians believe that Devenish could still be hiding an older pagan history. Long before the time of St Molaise, it was known as the Island of Learned Men and is thought to be the site of a Druid-led university.

The Sperrin Mountains,
Co Tyrone (previous
page); the intricate stone
cross and mysterious
round tower on
Devenish Island.

The mother of all Irish yews
❭ FLORENCE COURT, COUNTY FERMANAGH

All across Ireland you come across the native yew, *Taxus baccata* 'Fastigiata', a compact, upright tree quite different from the bushy, sprawling English yew. However, every one of the millions of the Irish form ('fastigiata' means upright) comes from a solitary, increasingly decrepit specimen growing in the park of Florence Court. Its story dates back to the 1770s when a tenant farmer by the name of George Willis was hunting in the lee of the nearby Cuilcagh mountains. His eye was caught by two curious upswept yews, the likes of which he had never seen before. Carefully, he dug them both out and returned them to his farm. One he planted near his house and the other he gave as a sign of goodwill to his landlord, the Earl of Enniskillen.

The original ageing yew tree at Florence Court (above); Florence Court seen from the south east (right).

How to get there:
Florence Court is found just off the A32 Swanlinbar road, 8 miles south west of Enniskillen. For sat nav users: BT92 1DB
Nearest railway station: Carrick-on-Shannon (36 miles)
Bus services:
www.translink.co.uk
028 9066 6630

Find out more:
www.nationaltrust.org.uk
028 6634 8249

John Craven on Northern Ireland's Lake District »

The warmth of the welcome you receive in County Fermanagh is just amazing and there are lots of fantastic little islands to explore on Lough Erne. There is also the annual Fermanagh Classic Fishing Festival, which has now been running for over 30 years. Even throughout the Troubles fishermen weren't put off travelling from all over the world to enjoy the festivities. I just love it – the relaxed atmosphere and, of course, the *craic* in the pubs!

While George's tree didn't survive the transplant, the Earl's thrived. Noted as a freak of nature, it became the talk of the horticultural world and many requested cuttings. By 1820 the tree was being commercially propagated and, by the end of the century, the 'Florence Court Yew' was one of the most popular trees in the country.

If you want to see this amazing progenitor, now is the time. The years are starting to take their toll on the Earl's original tree and, although the estate contains many of its descendants, this is a piece of history that is literally dying before your eyes.

Other things to see:
The grand 18th-century house dominates the Florence Court estate, now maintained by the National Trust. There is a working sawmill, powered by a water mill, and delightful gardens, best seen in spring when the daffodils are in full bloom.

Matt Baker on an eye-opening canoe trail »

Strangford Lough is the biggest sea inlet in the British Isles and what better way to explore it than by taking to a canoe? When Julia and I visited the Lough to find out more about its unique tidal-energy scheme, I went on a brand-new canoe trail, ending up on Salt Island. Once farmed by the Victorians the island is now maintained by the National Trust and is a great place to go camping. There's even Northern Ireland's very first bothy, which was until recently run down and vandalised. Now, the sheep that often sheltered there have been moved out so that campers can move in. The trail covers 80 square nautical miles and certainly opened up stunning landscape that I'd never experienced before.

Sea power

❯ STRANGFORD LOUGH, COUNTY DOWN

Strangford Lough is the largest sea inlet in the British Isles, covering 58 square miles. Much of it is still, calm water over vast mudflats except for the five-mile long fast-flowing tidal narrows where the lough is connected to the Irish Sea by Strangford Narrows. Almost completely landlocked by 150 miles of coastline of little bays, rocky outcrops, marshes and headlands, the lough contains 120 islands and its importance for wildlife is recognised internationally.

It supports over 2,000 marine animals and plants, including 72 per cent of all species recorded around the coast of Northern Ireland. The waters that sweep through the 500-metre wide gap that connects the inlet to the sea are rich in the plankton, shrimp and crabs that attract porpoises, seals and otters to the lough, while around 7,000 birds overwinter on the sands and mudflats.

Strangford Lough is also the location for some unique technology, which is leading the way in green, sustainable energy. SeaGen operates like an underwater windmill. However, it is not the wind that spins its twin rotors, but strong tidal currents that can rush in and out of the lough at speeds of up to eight knots. The tidal generators harvest enough energy to power a thousand homes. The advantage of marine turbines such as these is that, unlike the wind, the tide is almost 100 per cent predictable.

The black and red turbine – which can be seen peeking out of the lough's surface – went online in 2008 and is part of a five-year project to test the validity of this new form of sustainable energy. Already, plans are under way to build a commercial tidal farm off the coast of Anglesey that would initial generate 10.5MW of clean, reliable energy from seven turbines.

Unsurprisingly, when the plans for the turbine were first announced, there was a small amount of local opposition. The company responsible for the turbine insisted that as its rotors only make 10–15rpm, it poses little danger to wildlife. An independent research committee was established to monitor the lough's environment, from changes in the seabed to special devices that record the underwater sounds to detect porpoise movements, giving scientists an unprecedented level of knowledge about life in the lough, including the previously unknown fact that its seal population is not resident all year round. Tracking devices reveal that the seals travel all over the waters around Britain.

How to get there:
Strangford Lough Wildlife Centre is a great place to start exploring the area. It is situated at Castle Ward, Downpatrick, off the Audleystown road. For sat nav users: BT30 7LS
Nearest railway station: Bangor (41 miles)
Bus services:
www.translink.co.uk
028 9066 6630

Find out more:
www.strangfordlough.org
028 4488 1411

Other things to see:
A visit to Exploris: The Northern Ireland Aquarium at Portaferry is a great way to discover more about the indigenous wildlife on Strangford Lough and to watch the seals at the sanctuary and hospital.
www.exploris.org.uk
028 4272 8062

Strangford village near Downpatrick, Strangford Lough.

The Mountains of Mourne sweep down to the sea

> ❯ THE MOUNTAINS OF MOURNE, COUNTY DOWN

How to get there:

Rostrevor is found on
the A2 Shore Road.
For sat nav users: BT34
(Rostrevor)
Nearest railway station:
Newry (9 miles)
Bus services:
www.translink.co.uk
028 9066 6630

Find out more:

www.walkni.com
028 9030 3930

The Cloughmore Stone.

The Mountains of Mourne offer some of the best walking any rambler could dream of, up there with the Lakes, Peak District and Scotland. One of the finest ways to explore the territory is to follow a small section of the 625-mile Ulster Way, a circular route that skirts around the entirety of Northern Ireland. The recently new and improved walk was the brainchild of Wilfred Capper back in the 1970s who was inspired after walking the Pennine Way. Over time, the walk fell into disuse after landowners began to refuse access over certain sections of the increasingly fragmented route. In 2003, the Environment Agency began redeveloping the Ulster Way, gaining access to private land and, if the original paths weren't available, opening new sections to complete the circuit. The final section of the route opened in 2009.

The 26-mile Mourne Way section follows the foothills of the 12 compact, but towering, mountains, including Northern Ireland's highest summit, the 852-metre Slieve Donard.

The walk begins at Rostrevor, a village on the edge of a forest of Douglas fir, pine and Sitka spruce, and throws in an early challenge. The Cloughmore Stone is a 40-tonne granite boulder left here 10,000 years ago, at the end of the last ice age. It's a steep hike up to the boulder but when you make it the effort expended in getting there is soon forgotten as you take in staggering views across forest and mountains.

Other things to see:
There are more classic walks with great views in the Mourne district including the Brandy Pad, a ramble along an 18th-century smugglers' path. It begins at the Bloody Bridge on the A2 coast road to Newcastle, the site of a massacre in 1641 where Magennises ambushed Presbyterian prisoners. The walk ends over seven miles away in Clonachullion Wood.

It's not only the views that will leave you impressed. Work began on the famous Mourne Wall in 1904. Eighteen years later it was completed. The reason why this drystone wall took so long to complete is that it runs for 22 miles, passing 15 mountains on its serpentine journey around the 3,642-hectare (9,000-acre) catchment area of the Silent Valley Reservoir.

The route continues through the beautiful Trassey Valley, where granite used to be quarried for export to Liverpool, and on into the 200-year-old Tollymore Forest. With some of the most spectacular trees in Ireland, including an avenue of ancient cedars, the forest is a haven for red squirrels. By controlling the greys and feeding the reds, conservationists have worked wonders here. In 2004 there were only 11 red squirrels within the forest with 33 greys. Four years later, the red population numbered over 100, while the greys had all but gone.

While it's tempting to sit and watch the squirrels scamper around their feeding stations all day, the sea is calling as the Mourne Way ends at Newcastle, the place where, as the 19th-century musician Percy French sang, 'The Mountains of Mourne sweep down to the sea.'

Hikers by the Mourne Wall on the way up Slieve Donard (above). A view across the Mountains of Mourne from the summit of Slieve Donard (overleaf).

A giant journey

❯ CAUSEWAY COASTAL ROUTE, COUNTY ANTRIM

How to get there:

This section of the route
starts at the Giant's Causeway,
Bushmills, in County Antrim.
For sat nav users: BT57 8SU
Nearest railway station:
Portrush (6 miles)
Bus services:
www.translink.co.uk
028 9066 6630

Find out more:

www.causewaycoastandglens.
com
028 7032 7720

A striking natural marvel,
the Giant's Causeway.

We're cheating a bit here. It's impossible to cover the entire Causeway Coastal Route in one perfect day. In fact, if you even try, you're cheating yourself. This country drive begins in Londonderry and follows the meandering coast 120 miles around to Belfast. Along the way you'll skirt all nine of Antrim's glorious glens, discover where Jonathan Swift, of *Gulliver's Travels* fame, practised as a minister, be able to sample the delights of the world's oldest licensed whiskey distillery and visit the only completely walled city in the British Isles. We're going to highlight just one section of it, the 37 miles between Limavady and our starting point, the Giant's Causeway.

According to legend the geological miracle of the Giant's Causeway was built by the Irish giant Finn MacCool so that he could nip across the ocean and beat up his Scottish rival Benandonner on the Isle of Staffa (see page 158). When he arrived and found his sleeping enemy he discovered that old Benan was about twice his size and fled back to Ireland in fear.

While it makes for a great fairytale, the reality is that the 40,000 interlocking hexagonal columns are the result of basaltic lava cracking when it cooled. If you've never been there, now is the time to see the Causeway. Climate change is taking its toll on the natural phenomenon that once ripped apart the Spanish Armada. The National Trust believes that, by 2020, access will be restricted with rising seas swamping the Causeway and making it dangerous to shipping.

If you head west along the Coastal Route from the Giant's Causeway you find Dunluce Castle, a late-medieval and 17th-century castle perched precariously on the north Antrim

cliffs. Besieged by Elizabethan forces in 1584, the castle suffered a tragedy 55 years later when storm conditions caused a section of the cliff to tumble into the raging sea beneath, plunging the castle kitchens and seven of their staff to their untimely end in the ocean.

Back in the car, your journey takes you past the cliff-top folly that is Mussenden Temple and the vast sandy beaches of Magilligan and Benone Strand. Your day ends with a visit to the Roe Valley Country Park, extending three miles on either side of the River Roe near Limavady, a favourite location for anglers, walkers and wildlife watchers. It is also where you find Northern Ireland's first domestic hydro-electric power station that until 1963 had provided environmentally friendly juice to houses in the locality for nearly 70 years.

Other things to see:

Head east instead of west from the Giant's Causeway and you'll come across the Carrick-a-Rede Rope Bridge at Ballintoy. Dare you walk over a 23-metre drop to reach the abundant birdlife on Carrick Island?

Carrick-a-Rede
Rope Bridge.

The new world

❯ ULSTER AMERICAN FOLK PARK, COUNTY TYRONE

During the 18th and 19th centuries Ulster, like the rest of Ireland, saw a mass exodus. Poverty, politics and the potato famine forced millions to turn their backs on their old life and head out to a brave new world: America. Between 1820 and 1880 3.5 million Irish men, women and children abandoned the Emerald Isle to embrace the Land of the Free.

You get an idea of how desperate these emigrants were when you step on board the *Brig Union*, a replica ship moored at the Ulster American Folk Park. Those seeking a way out paid anything between £4 and £10 to squeeze on board the 30-metre long vessel for the journey across the Atlantic to the Big Apple. The often hazardous crossing could take anything up to 12 weeks – a long time to find yourself crammed between decks with 200 other emigrants. To help you appreciate how awful conditions were, this superb museum has even gone so far as to throw in a few foul stenches within the claustrophobic berths.

How to get there:

The museum is open Tues–Sun throughout the year and can be found on the A5 between Omagh and Strabane.
For sat nav users: BT78 5QU
Nearest railway station:
Londonderry (30 miles)
Bus services:
www.translink.co.uk
028 9066 6630

Find out more:

www.nmni.com

028 8224 3292

Other things to see:

The museum is situated near one of Northern Ireland's least-explored areas – the Sperrins, a rugged landscape of mountains, open water and bog. The 9-mile Robbers Table walk gives you spectacular views of the High Sperrin and Bluestack ranges from an area once plagued by bands of rapparee (or highwaymen). A route can be downloaded for free at www.walkni.com. There are also scenic cycling and driving routes to follow.

A view of Gortin Lakes, looking north east over the Sperrins range.

The *Brig* is just one of the attractions at the open-air museum. There are over 30 buildings here, all giving you a clue as to why so many Irish uprooted in the first place and what life was like when they arrived in their new home.

As you wander around the Park it's quickly apparent that some emigrants did better than others. The replica six-bedroom Pennsylvania Farmhouse, based on the original constructed by one Thomas Mellon, is a mansion compared to the cramped two-room log cabin that his family first moved into on their arrival in America in 1819. The Mellons were lucky: they prospered and started to move up in the world; while others never progressed from these early log shacks.

With a number of permanent and special exhibitions throughout the year, this is an intriguing window into a fascinating period of Irish history.

The cow fort
▶ BELLAGHY BAWN, COUNTY LONDONDERRY

The 1611 Plantation of Ulster was the most audacious programme of colonisation ever undertaken by the English in an effort to force the Gaelic chiefs to submit to the rule of James I. Six Ulster counties would be cleared of the native Irish and replaced by English and Scots. However, the settlers arriving in Ireland soon realised that their new home wasn't everything they had been led to expect. They found themselves living in fear of the 'woodkerne', displaced Irishmen who were living rough, ready to attack new settlements at every opportunity.

To secure the finance needed for such a massive colonisation, the English Crown turned to 12 London Companies who would become the landlords of this new territory. The companies protected their assets with the construction of bawns, or fortified buildings.

The Irish bawn got its name from two Gaelic words: *Ba* meaning 'cattle', and *Dhun* from 'fort'. Badhuns, or over time, bawns, were built all over Ulster to protect the property of the companies. The houses were usually located in the middle of a courtyard, protected by walls of stone, clay, timber or sod.

The Bellaghy Bawn is one of the most famous. The building was commissioned in 1614 by John Rowley, the then agent of the Vintners Company of London, the main landholders in the Londonderry Plantation. When Rowley died just three years later, another agent, Baptist Jones, was transferred from a local project to finish the work. It wasn't a good move. Jones himself died six years later leaving considerable debts. The Vintners Company duly appointed a new leaseholder, Henry Conway, who not only assumed Jones' position but also took on his debts and even married his widow.

It wasn't long before the bawn's defences were tested – and found wanting. In 1641 Irish rebels laid siege to the village and Conway hurriedly brought his tenants into the courtyard. While this seemed a noble act, Conway then made a deal with the Irish and fled with his family, leaving the settlers to the mercy of the locals. The bawn was burnt to the ground. The red-bricked bawn was rebuilt in 1643, with a new house added in 1791. The now white-washed stronghold was opened to the public in 1996 and is home to various exhibitions about the dark days of the plantations and the wonderful natural history of Lough Beg.

How to get there:

Bellaghy Bawn is open Wed–Sun. It is two miles off the main Belfast to Londonderry road, on the B182, just off the A54.

For sat nav users: BT45 8LA

Nearest railway station: Cullybackey (11½ miles)

Bus services:

www.translink.co.uk

028 9066 6630

Find out more:

www.ni-environment.gov.uk

028 7938 6812

Other things to see:

Nobel prize-winning poet Seamus Heaney was born in Bellaghy and its bawn houses a library devoted to his work, including his manuscripts, books, broadcasts – even his old school bag is on display. Guided tours include a special film about the area by Heaney himself and a collection of other contemporary Irish writers' work.

Bellaghy Bawn house.

› Index

❯ Picture acknowledgements

BBC Books would like to thank the following individuals and organisations for providing photographs and for permission to reproduce copyright material. While every effort has been made to trace and acknowledge copyright holders, we should like to apologise should there be any errors or omissions. Abbreviations: l left, r right, tl top left, tr top right, bl bottom left, br bottom right.

Page 1 Stephen Dorey/Alamy; pp2-3 Peter Lewis/Oxford Scientific; p6 Rod Edward/Britain on View/Photolibrary; p7 Lee Beel/Britain on View/Photolibrary; p9 Adam Burton/The Travel Library/Photolibrary; p10 BSH Stock/Alamy; p11 Ellen Rooney/Robert Harding Travel; pp12-13 Derek Croucher/Britain on View/ Photolibrary; p14 Peter Barritt/Alamy; p17 Craig Joiner Photography/Alamy; p18 Adam Burton/Britain on View/Photolibrary; p20 tl John Glover/Alamy, br Adam Burton/Britain on View/Photolibrary; p21 Roy Westlake/Imagestate RM/Photolibrary; pp22-23 Patrick Ward/Corbis; p24 John Harper/Corbis; p25 Jack Sullivan/Alamy; p26 Paul Quayle/Axiom; p27 Jason Hawkes/Corbis; p29 Jason Hawkes; p30 Neville Stanikk/Cornish Picture Library; p31 David Lyons/Alamy; p33 Alistair Laming/ Alamy; p35 MMGI Marianne Majerus; p37 Jason Hawkes; p39 Jergenija Piqozne/Imagebroker.net/Photolibrary; p41 NTPL/Britain on View/Photolibrary; p43 l and r Jason Hawkes; p44 Adrian Warren/Dae Sasitorn/lastrefuge.co.uk; p46 David Kirk/The East Grinstead Society; p47 Raf Makda/View Pictures/Photolibrary; p49 Angela Hampton Picture Library/Alamy; p50 David Sellman/Britain on View/Photolibrary; p51 Andy Williams/The Travel Library/Photolibrary; p52 tl Rod Edwards/Britain on View/Photolibrary, r John Miller/Britain on View/Photolibrary; p54 John Wade/Alamy; p55 Mirror Pix/Trinity Mirror/Alamy; p57 Rod Edwards/Photolibrary; pp58-59 Homer Sykes/Country Collection/Alamy; p60 Britain on View/Photolibrary; p61 E. A. James/age fotostock/Photolibrary; p62 Martin Pope/Telegraph; p63 Danny Greeu/rspb-images.com; p64 Roy Rainford/Robert Harding Travel; p65 Rupert Truman/NTPL; p66 Hiroshi Shimura; p68 tl Jeremy Pardoe/Alamy, br Keith Vaughan Pritchard/TIPS Italia/Photolibrary; p69 Alan Spencer Norfolk/Alamy; p70 Clay Perry/Corbis; p71 Country Life; p72 Joe Cornish/NTPL; p73 Richard Bowden/Alamy; p74 Superstock Inc/Photolibrary; p75 t look-foto/H&D Zieiskel/ Photolibrary, b David Levenson/NTPL; p77 Cephas Picture Library/Alamy; p78 Peter Scholey/Robert Harding Travel; p81 t Fran Haisall/Britain on View/Photolibrary, b Simon Woodcock/Alamy; p82 Colin Underhill/Alamy; p83 David Hunter/Britain on View/Photolibrary; p84 Mike Hayward/Photoshropshire.com/Alamy; p85 Charles Leventon; p86 Claire Carter; p87 Britain on View/Photolibrary; p88 David Jones/Alamy; p89 soundimageplus/Alamy; pp90-91 Neil Phillips/Cephas Picture Library/Alamy; p92 t Doug Blake/Alamy, b NRT – Helena/Alamy; p93 Haydn West/Press Association; pp94-95 Robin Bush/Oxford Scientific/Photolibrary; p97 Stephen Dorey/Alamy; p98 Rex Features; p101 John Grimshaw/Colesbourne Park; p102 Andreas von Einsiedel/NTPL; p103 Richard Croft; p104 David J. Green/Alamy; p105 David Tipling/ rspb-images.com; p107 Robert Conley/Alamy; p108 Pawel Libera/Britain on View/Photolibrary; p109 Roger Coulam/Alamy; pp110-111 Andrew Curtis; pp112-113 Kielder Partnership; p114 Adrian Warren/Dae Sasitorn/Lastrefuge.co.uk; p115 Bill Lockhart; p116 Tom Parker/Pictures of Britain; p117 Stuart Kelly/ Alamy; p118 DGB/Alamy; p119 Nicholas Hawksmoor/Skyscan/Corbis; p120 Britain on View/Photolibrary; p121 Graeme-Peacock.com; p122 Wojtex Buss/age fotostock/Photolibrary; p123 Country Life; pp124-125 Andy Stothert/Britain on View/Photolibrary; p125 Mike Kipling/Alamy; p126 Andy Williams/The Travel Library/Photolibrary; p127 Edward Nurse; p128 Will Wintercroft; p129 Yorkshire Post/Ross Parry Syndication; p131 Jon Sparks; p132 Marga Werner/age footstock/ Photolibrary; p133 Rod Edwards/Alamy; p135 NTPL/Britain on View/Photolibrary; p136 Ben Barden/Alamy; p137 Adrian Warren/lastrefuge.co.uk; pp138-139 Val Corbett/Britain on View/Photolibrary; p140 Rob Watkins/Alamy; p141 Dave Willis; pp142-143 English Heritage/Imagestate RM/Photolibrary; p145 Graham Cooper/ Pennineimages.com; p146 Jon Sparks; p147 James Leonard/Cyanens Photography; p149 Alan Nevelli/Alamy; p150 Pete Seaward/Britain on View/Photolibrary; pp152-153 Neale Clark/Robert Harding Travel; p155 John Maddrell/IOM Newspapers; p157 Norma Joseph/Alamy; p159 Tony Waltham/Robert Harding Travel; p160 Raymond Wardenaer; pp162-163 Andy Stothert/Britain on View/Photolibrary; pp164-165 Frost Lee/Imagestate RM/Photolibrary; p167 l Cotswolds Photo Library/Britain on View/Photolibrary, r dbphots/Alamy; p168 Derek Croucher/Britain on View/Photolibrary; p169 Don Bishop/The Travel Library/Photolibrary; pp170-171 Dennis Barnes/Britain on View/Photolibrary; p173 l John McKenna/Alamy, r Tom Mackie/Alamy; p174 Jam World Images/Alamy; p175 Rob Gray; p176 Don Brownlow/Alamy; p177 Findlay Rankin/Britain on View/Photolibrary; p178 Iain Sarjeant/Oxford Scientific/Photolibrary; p179 Simon Ledingham/ Visitcumbria.com; p181 Lovely Light/Alamy; p182 Flight Images LLP/Britain on View/Photolibrary; p183 Graham Lawrence/Alamy; p184 Claire Carter; pp186-187 Claire Carter; p188 Chris Warren/Loop Images; p189 Colin Palmer Photography/Alamy; p191 Jeremy Moore/Alamy; p192 Cered.org; p193 Martin Barlow/ The Photo Library Wales/Alamy; p194 GeoPictures.net; Simon Kitchin/Landscape Photographyuk.com; p196 The Photolibrary Wales/Photolibrary; p197 Barry Batchelor/ Press Association Images; p198 Ian Richards ABIPP Pembrokeshire Photography; p199 Claire Carter; p201 David Angel/Britain on View/Photolibrary; pp202-203 Chris Warren/Superstock/Photolibrary; pp204-205 Air Images Ltd/aerialphotography.com; p207 The Irish Image Collection/Design Pics Inc/Photolibrary; p209 The Irish Image Collection/Photolibrary; p210 Peter Muhly/National Trust; pp210-211 National Trust Photo Library/Britain on View/Photolibrary; pp212 and 214 The Irish Image Collection/Photolibrary; p215 Eoin Clarke/Lonely Planet Images; pp216-217 Gareth McCormack/Alamy; p218 Britain on View/ Photolibrary; p219 Japan Travel Bureau/Photolibrary; p220 Chris Hill/Scenicireland.com; p221 Joefox County Derry/Alamy.